DEDICATION

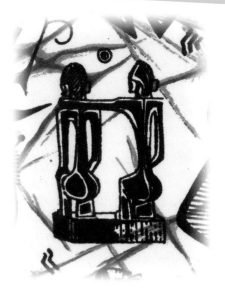

"A person is a person through other persons."
—Bantu proverb

This book is dedicated to the incomparable textile artists of The Continent, whose names are not known to us, but whose artistry, skill, and ingenuity continue to inspire us all in new and exciting ways.

ACKNOWLEDGMENTS

This project would not be possible without the help and support of many people. In particular, I wish to thank:

Paul and Wandra Shepard, whose beautiful home in Maryland was used for the on-location photography. The warmth, comfort, and style created by their African antiques and furnishings provided the perfect backdrop for African Accents. Thank you for the use of your house and so much more.

Sylvia and LeRoy Shepard for their endless support, patience, and enthusiasm and unlimited availability. My appreciation for you goes beyond words.

Wayne Partlow, my on-location photographer, whose skill, sense of humor, and professionalism are a rare and wonderful combination.

Cindy Noren, Vandarra Robbins, and Sylvia Shepard for providing technical assistance and demonstrating the fabric techniques in the first chapter.

The companies whose fabrics and craft supplies are used in the book. Thank you for sharing your information and quality products: Homeland Authentics, HTC, Inc., AfriCraft, One World Button Supply Company, Kreinik, Home Arts, Calico Moon Handcrafts, Design I, Liquitex, Mission Valley Textiles, Inc., Beacon Adhesives/Signature Crafts, Aleene's, Viking Sewing Machine Company, Walnut Hollow, Loose Ends, Rubber Stampede, Fiber City Sewing, Chronicle Books, The Crowning Touch, The Unique Spool, Dharma Trading, and Bag Works.

Moses Coulibaly, Abdoulaye Diaw, Jacki Robinson, Jacquie Thomas, Barbara Stewart, Judi Kauffman, Clare Smith, Ronke Luke-Boone, Duncan Clarke, Herman Smalls, and Dusty Rhodes for their various contributions to the book.

Meadowlands Photo Service and LeRoy Shepard for the cover photography.

The people at Krause Publications, including my editor Amy Tincher-Durik and the rest of the team. You are truly a pleasure to work with.

My treasured family and friends who have offered ideas, vibes, encouragement, assistance, meals, and the peace and quiet I needed to complete this project.

TABLE OF CONTENTS

When you think of "African fabrics," what probably comes to mind first are the familiar cotton prints with bold gold accents, vibrant geometrics, or printed designs that mimic true woven kente cloth. Yet, as beautiful as these are, it's important to remember that the category takes in an entire continent of creativity. Each fiber technique carries great significance for its particular region of The Continent; each is a mode of creative expression, social and political communication, and economic endeavor. As such, the value of textile arts in African cultures can't be overestimated.

The visual excitement of Africa's colors, textures, and patterns is increasingly sought after in the home decor market worldwide, from upholstered furniture to the many African-inspired lines of bed, bath, and kitchen linens, window treatments, and

other textile products now available. Continued globalization also gives rise to eclectic, culturally diverse interior design, mixing a variety of influences. The way we decorate our surroundings has become one of the most meaningful expressions of our individualism, and African fabrics bring a unique character to the home, at the same time conveying comfort, drama, and a certain timelessness.

Throughout Africa, objects that are found in the home are created to serve a dual purpose, that is, combining function with beauty. Even the simplest utilitarian pieces, such as spoons, bowls, and containers, are carved or otherwise treated to give a special aesthetic quality to everyday life. It's no wonder African influences are so apparent in the works of Matisse, Picasso, and other world-renowned artists.

Part of the fun of working with the wide array of African fabrics is discovering the rich cultural aspects tied into the various designs and processes. With the exception of raffia fabrics from Zaire in central Africa, the fabrics presented here are of West African origin, including Ghanaian kente strip weaving and adinkra stamping, Korhogo designs of the Ivory Coast, and bogolanfini (mudcloth) from Mali. Designs often carry specific meanings, with certain fabrics being reserved for special purposes. These works of art are the result of relatively simple means and materials, coupled with labor-intensive methods. They are a testament to the resourcefulness of the artisans as much as their creativity.

My fascination with African fabrics grew out of a combined interest in sewing and African art in general. I returned from a trip to Senegal in 1986 with an "instant collection" that still continues to expand, piece by piece. Most of the pieces are used for home decor rather than apparel sewing. By decorating with them, I can enjoy my mudcloths, korhogos, prints, and kuba cloths every day and share them with others. See how well these fabrics mix with other styles that appeal to you for a truly personalized home environment. I blend them with touches of Indian and Indonesian design; the similarity of colors (deep reds, blacks with golds, and muted earth tones) and dramatic motifs (like geometric and nature figures) ties these styles together in an interesting way. I hope that this book inspires you to create useful, beautiful African Accents and helps you to understand the significance behind the fabrics.

Lisa Shepard

www.CulturedExpressions.com

ABOUT THIS BOOK

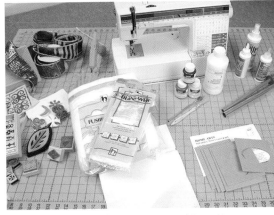

The first chapter explains the authentic methods used to make African fabrics and provides instructions for re-creating some similar looks with readily available materials. Note that the instructions given are intended as fun, creative exercises and are not intended to replace the real thing, but try using your own versions of the fabrics as well as the authentics in creating the projects. It's my hope that as you learn about the processes involved, you'll gain a deeper appreciation for the authentic African textiles and begin to collect and enjoy them for years to come.

The chapters that follow present the fabrics and trims used in home decor projects. Although each chapter covers a different room in the home, most of the projects can be used in other rooms just as easily. Some projects require basic sewing, while others can be completed with a household iron and no-sew fusibles, a glue gun, staple gun, or a combination of these.

Some of the tools and supplies used in creating African Accents.

With these ideas as a starting point, let your own creativity guide you in working through the projects, from your choice of fabric to the end uses. Use them for accents in your own home as well as unique gift items for others. Some of the projects are suitable for children to complete, making them perfect for family activities and classroom use. I would suggest that for each project you want to try, you **read through the instructions completely before you begin, to get yourself familiar with the techniques and materials needed.**

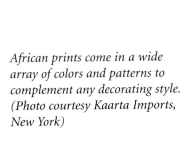

African prints come in a wide array of colors and patterns to complement any decorating style. (Photo courtesy Kaarta Imports, New York)

Because authentic mudcloth and korhogos are handcrafted, the sizes of the cloths will vary and are difficult to measure in exact yards. You can expect to pay from $25 per piece and up for these fabrics. True woven kente can range from $15 to $50 per strip, or from a few hundred dollars for full cloths made of many strips sewn together. By comparison, the familiar printed kente designs are similar in price to other cotton craft fabrics, from about $5 per yard. Kuba fabrics can start at around $30 per piece. All of these prices are approximate and will vary according to the source, the fabric's quality, and the complexity of design. Note that African specialty shops are an excellent source for the fabrics, as are fabric stores and vendors found at African festivals and expos. These should generally offer lower prices than art galleries and museum gift shops.

If you can't find them locally, the Resource section lists various sources for the fabrics, buttons, ribbons, and trims used throughout the book. In addition, craft and sewing supply manufacturers are listed; contact them for local retailer information or, in some cases, to order supplies directly. You can further your enjoyment and study of African fabrics and related subjects by referring to the Bibliography as well as the reference books, museums, Internet sites, and other resources.

(Photo courtesy Kaarta Imports, New York)

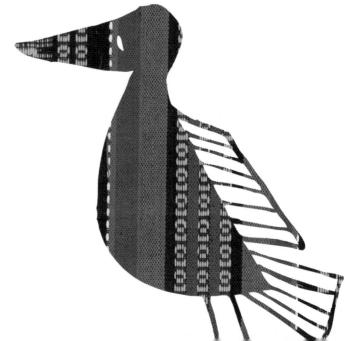

Chapter One

TECHNIQUES

The handwork involved in African fabrics is part of what makes them so striking! Because the artisans weave, paint, or stitch them one piece at a time, no two pieces are alike. By studying the fabrics closely, you can easily imagine the seemingly effortless motions of a textile maker at work.

Once you've become familiar with these looks, you'll begin to notice how often they're used in your favorite home decor publications, successfully blended with other design styles, from modern high-tech to Far Eastern to rustic country influences.

Each technique is described to give you an indication of the steps involved in creating them, followed by tips on recreating your own version of the look, using materials that are readily available in craft and fabric stores. The do-it-yourself instructions are offered as creative alternatives designed to approximate the general look of the original fabrics, not as replacements for them. Traditionally, these fabrics are the result of methods that require years of apprenticeship, as well as materials that are indigenous to a specific area (for instance certain tree barks and leaves or natural dyes.). As such, step-by-step directions are not divulged to outsiders. In trying the simplified versions, you are sure to appreciate the time-honored workmanship of the original artisans that much more.

When making your own versions, remember that perfection doesn't have to be the goal, because you're striving for a handcrafted look. If you think you've made a mistake, such as an adinkra misprint, or a drop of paint on a korhogo panel, look for ways to work around it or even incorporate it into the design. Sometimes this kind of "creative challenge" opens you up to new ideas you wouldn't have dreamed of otherwise.

Sources for most of the materials used are listed in the Resources section at the end of the book. Contact the companies for direct ordering information or for the names of local retailers.

Read through all of the instructions completely before you begin a technique and be sure to test your materials for the desired effects before you do the actual project.

Top to bottom: mudcloths in brick red and gold; kente cloth; korhogo panel; Kuba raffia velvet; pieced and embroidered raffia.

Covered in this chapter:

⬦ ADINKRA ⬦ KORHOGO ⬦
⬦ BOGOLANFINI (MUDCLOTH) ⬦
⬦ APPLIQUÉD KUBA CLOTH ⬦
⬦ EMBROIDERED KASAÏ VELVET ⬦
⬦ KENTE STRIP WEAVING ⬦

(Photo courtesy Aid to Artisans)

Adinkra

Adinkra stamping is a printing process of the Ashanti people of Ghana. It traces back to at least the beginning of the 19th century, and probably earlier. The designs were originally printed on deep red or black fabric and worn by mourners at funerals as a gesture of respect for the ancestors, for the word *adinkra*, or *adinkera*, means "good-bye."

Adinkra stamps are carved from calabashes (gourds), with the raised areas becoming the print surface for each symbol. Usually, sticks are arranged on top of the stamp in tripod fashion for easier handling.

The dyes are made from the peeled bark of badee trees. After soaking in water, the bark is pounded, then boiled in the same water. The boiling process is repeated several times over a week, with the addition of iron ore nuggets during the last few boilings. The iron turns the dye a deep black color. Egg white is also added to the cooled dyestuff to give it a glossy finish, providing contrast when stamped onto plain black fabric. The consistency of the dye is thick and paste-like, similar to tar.

What makes the dye-making process remarkable is the fact that what begins as a 5-gallon vat of ingredients literally boils down to yield only about a half-gallon of dyestuff. Imagine such a laborious process that results in ten percent of what you started with!

Once the precious dye is ready, the artist prepares the cloth by drawing horizontal and vertical lines across it with a wooden comb. These grid lines form frames and borders for the designs. The stamps are then dipped in the thick dye and pressed onto the fabric.

When the stamping is completed, the fabric is allowed to dry in the sun. Although it can be used as soon as it is thoroughly dried, true adinkra becomes washable only after being exposed to light and air for at least one year.

Finished cloths can repeat a single symbol throughout, or feature several different ones. Each symbol has a specific meaning, often derived from proverbs or historical events. Today, adinkra cloth is printed in a variety of colors for everyday wear. You can find the designs on solid fabrics as well as tie-dyed backgrounds. In Ghana, the wearing of adinkra signifies the wearer's preference for traditional over Western clothing. It also communicates one's status as a proud Ashanti.

(Photo courtesy Gold Coast Africa, Inc.)

Traditional adinkra cloth can repeat a single motif in a simple color scheme…

(Photo courtesy Duncan Clarke)

…Or feature a mix of patterns. In the garments above and at left, the stamped fabric strips are joined with brightly colored hand embroidery.

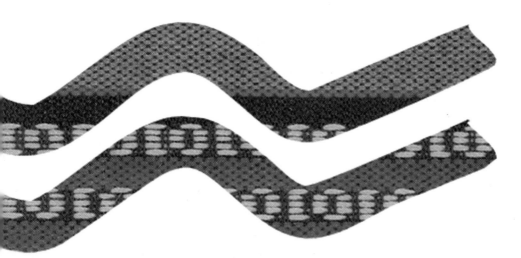

Try Adinkra Stamping

It's easy to approximate the look of adinkra cloth, especially given the popularity of rubber stamping to decorate fabric, paper, wood, and more. Choose your designs to suit a particular occasion, or to communicate a message. The place cards (page 60) and greeting cards (page 106) were made with rubber stamps, while the adinkra sampler pillow (page 78) and lampshade (page 94) were done with hand-cut compressed sponge stamps.

Directions for this adinkra pillow can be found in Chapter Five (page 78).

You'll Need

- Acrylic paints*
- Surface for stamping (fabric, cards, etc.)
- 1/2 potato for each stamp, a compressed sponge, or rubber stamps
- Plastic plates for paint mixing
- Optional: A textile medium should be added to the paints if stamping onto fabric
- Small paint brushes, small craft knife (or vegetable peeler or paring knife), popsicle sticks, sharp scissors, newspaper or plastic drop cloth, fine-line felt-tip pen

*Black, red, blue, green, yellow, and metallic gold were used in project shown

To Make Stamps

Note: Potato and rubber stamps give a more solid printed image, while a sponge will have a more mottled or antiqued effect. The surface you're stamping onto (whether it's smooth like sanded wood, or more textured like a very coarse cotton or burlap) will also affect the results. Test each to help you decide the best stamping method for your project. Also, keep in mind that whatever you carve will appear in reverse when stamped.

A compressed sponge prints a more mottled, "weathered" image than the smoother, fuller coverage of the potato stamp.

Potato Stamps

1. Cover your work area with newspaper or drop cloth. Wash potatoes thoroughly and cut each in half. Blot the potatoes with paper towel to remove any excess moisture. Draw designs freehand onto the cut side of the potato, or photocopy the designs shown on pages 15-17, cut them out, and place them on the potatoes, using them as patterns to trace around. Use a fine-line felt-tip marker to minimize bleeding of the lines.

Far left: After cutting the potato, blot the surface of the potato before drawing in the symbol to minimize bleeding of the ink.

Left: Once the larger areas are cut away, carve closer with a small knife for better control and a clearer printed image.

2. Cut away potato from the background areas of the design, cutting about 1/4" to 1/2" deep into the potato. For inner detail areas, use the tip of a vegetable peeler, paring knife, or craft knife to carve out the design. Stick a fork into the potato for easy handling.

Compressed Sponge Stamps

1. Photocopy the desired adinkra designs (pages 15-17) and use a rub-off technique to transfer the designs to the sponge. Rub the back of the paper with a pencil, then place the paper face-up on top of the compressed sponge sheet. Trace over the lines of the design to transfer them to the sponge. You can also draw the designs freehand onto the sponge sheets. Cut out the designs using sharp scissors.

Left: A compressed sponge is easy to trace on and cut.

2. After cutting the sponge designs out, wet them to expand the sponge. Squeeze out excess water. Attach a safety pin through the top of the sponge for easy handling when stamping.

Authentic adinkra dye is usually near-black in color. Mix red with green, then add black a drop at a time for the desired shade. For a more custom look, experiment and mix paints to achieve colors to match your decor. Add textile medium to paints if you're stamping onto fabric. The textile medium will keep the paint from stiffening the fabric and allow for better paint penetration into the fabric.

If an image stamps less than perfectly, fill it in using a small paint brush, rather than re-stamping over it.

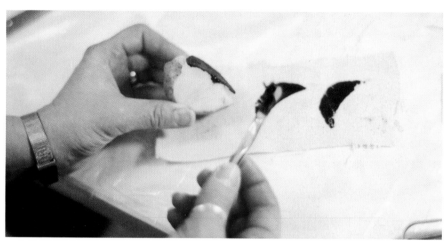

The best images are achieved by stamping on a hard surface (table, floor, etc.), padded slightly with newspapers. For the most authentic look, begin by painting the grid lines which separate the adinkra stamp designs, as shown. Use a small paintbrush to apply paints to the stamps, then try a few practice stampings on scrap fabric or paper. (Make your test pieces large enough to use in a different, smaller project; if you like the practice results, these tests won't go to waste!) Make any necessary adjustments to the cut design. Stamp onto your project surface. If an area doesn't print well, fill it in with a fine paintbrush rather than trying to re-stamp it. When the design is completed, allow it to dry thoroughly before handling.

Some of the many adinkra symbols are given here, with their names in Twi language followed by the translation or meaning behind each one.

KRAMO BONE AMMA YANHU KRAMO PA:
Signifies the difficulty in distinguishing the fake
from the genuine. A warning against hypocrisy.

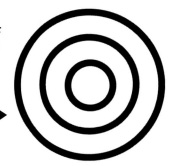

ADINKRAHENE: Chief (king) of all
adinkra designs.

DWANIMEM: Ram's horn design. Exemplifies
strength of body, mind, and spirit.

MPUANNUM: Five tufts design. A tradi-
tional hairstyle symbolic of beauty among
women.

NKONSONKONSO: Link or chain design.
Those who share blood relations never break
apart. Unity and interdependence.

ANANSE NTONTAN: The spider web.
Symbol of creativity and craftiness.

GYAMU ATIKO: Signifies the wartime bravery
and valor of Gyaku, an Ashante king.
A shaved hairstyle.

KEERAPA: A sign of sanctity and good
fortune.

OSRAN: The moon. The moon does not go around the earth quickly. Suggests patience and determination. ◀

ABAN: Sign of the fence. The mark of safety and protection. ▶

OWO FORO ADOBE: A snake climbing the palm tree. Represents the performing of an unusual or impossible task. ◀

BIRIRI WO SORO: A symbol of hope and optimism. ▶

NSOROMA: Symbol of the star (a child of the heavens) and a dependence upon the Supreme Being. ◀

SANKOFA: It is not taboo to return and correct your mistakes. Learning from the past. ▶

NKYIN KYIN: Changing one's self among various roles; adaptability. ◀

GYE NYAME: A figure of the omnipotence and immortality of the Supreme Being. ▶

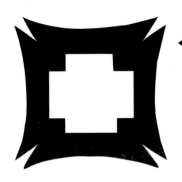

FIHANKRA: Signifies safety and security of the home.

ODENKYEM: The crocodile lives in water, but breathes air. Stresses the qualities propriety and prudence.

DONO NTOASO: The double drum sign symbolizes goodwill and alertness.

OHENE NIWA: The king sees everything, nothing escapes him. Sign of protection and vigilance.

MMRA KRADO: The seal of the court. A sign of authority and legitimacy of the law.

Some translations courtesy Bandele Publications (see Special Resources)

Korhogo

Korhogo cloth is a specialty of the Senufo people (made primarily by men) in the Ivory Coast. Natural-color spun cotton is loosely woven into narrow strips, about 4" wide. These are then sewn together by hand to make a larger piece of fabric. The cloth is then decorated with large handpainted figures of masked dancers, animals, birds, reptiles, and fish. Designs extend across the boundaries of the individual strips. Smaller geometric patterns are also sometimes included. The large size of the figures was intended to blend in with foliage, helping to camouflage the hunters who wore korhogo. Symbolically, it also protected these secret society members from harm, because the animal figures originally held spiritual significance. Today, the cloth is produced primarily for the tourist trade in a range of dye colors, from black to brown to rust-red.

Often, two dyes are used to create the painted figures. First, a dark green dyestuff is created by boiling the leaves and stems of bushes several times over. The second dye is a fermented, iron-rich mud base, collected from nearby swampy regions. After it is sifted through and thinned out with water, the mud dye is ready for use. It is the fermentation that causes the mud to act as a mordant, giving the final product some degree of lightfastness and washability, and it causes the first dye to take on an even deeper color.

Directions for this korhogo floorcloth can be found in Chapter Two (page 47).

Working on the ground, the korhogo painter stretches the blank cotton and pins it to a board. He outlines the major figures and the larger details as basic line drawings across the cloth using a dull blade. The design is then filled in with other tools, such as a small brush. A variety of brushstrokes is used for the fill patterns, giving a unique "texture" to each figure. Some of the fill patterns employed include short thick vertical lines, herringbones, long thin lines, feathery strokes, diagonals, crosshatching, dots, checkered designs, and solid areas.

Try Korhogo Painting

The dramatic look of korhogo lends itself to a bare wall or floor. It can even be cut strategically to showcase single motifs for pillow fronts, apparel, quilt blocks, and other smaller applications. The room divider (page 43), floorcloth (page 47), and bulletin board (page 92) were created with authentic korhogo panels.

You'll Need

- Approx. 1-1/2 yards off-white, loosely-woven cotton or cotton canvas
- Acrylic paints*
- Textile medium
- Dull craft knife or popsicle stick for outlining
- Paint brushes in two or three sizes for fill patterns and detailing
- Fusible hem tape
- Iron, newspaper or plastic drop cloth

*Black, red, and green were used in the project shown

1. A realistic-looking korhogo can be achieved by cutting the fabric horizontally into 5" strips, then restitching them by hand or machine using a 1/2" seam allowance. For a clean finish, turn under 1" on all sides of the fabric and hem using a straight machine stitch, or do a no-sew hem using fusible hem tape such as Stitch Witchery or Trans Web. To use the korhogo as a wall hanging, turn under 3" at the top edge, forming a rod pocket for a curtain rod or tree branch to fit through.

2. Spread out newspapers or a plastic dropcloth to protect your work surface. If desired, secure the fabric with weights placed along the edges to help keep it taut and flat as you paint; heavy cans or bricks will work well. Select some of the motifs shown on pages 20 and 21, combining elements of these to create your own designs. Consider changing the fill patterns from those shown to make the motifs even more unique.

3. Make the "dye" color you want by mixing red with green, then adding a drop of black at a time as desired. Blending your color in this way will create shades of off-black, browns, or deep reds that are more realistic (and easier on the eye) than using pure black paint. Add textile medium and a bit of water to thin the paint slightly so the cotton fabric will absorb it more easily. Test colors on a fabric scrap before you begin.

4. Dip the craft knife or popsicle stick into the paint and outline the designs on the fabric. (Although the korhogo artists do this freehand, it's okay to roughly sketch out the placement of your figures lightly in pencil first if you want to.) Next, fill in the designs with patterns like those shown. Let dry.

Above: Korhogo motifs are mostly simple geometric shapes, which makes them fun and easy to draw. It might be helpful to outline them first very lightly in pencil before you paint the outlines.

Far left: Popsicle sticks are perfect for outlining your design.

Left: Korhogo designs make a great project for kids and adults alike!

Bogolanfini (Mudcloth)

Authentic mudcloth comes primarily in shades of black and brown, but you'll also find more vibrant tones of brick red, jade, burnt orange, gold, and more.

Mudcloth is the more commonly known name for bogolanfini, a technique of the Bamana people of Mali in West Africa. The making of mudcloth is a skill that is traditionally passed on from mother to daughter. Like various other African fabrics, its bold designs are inspired by everyday objects as well as proverbs and historical events. It was primarily worn by girls in rights-of-passage events and by hunters for the common goal of protection from malevolent forces.

For all of its artistic value and graphic appeal, however, mudcloth's popularity worldwide is relatively new. Until the 1970s, the cloth had only local appeal in Mali, among its more rural people. In fact, mudcloth was long despised by the region's more educated urban-dwellers, who considered it anything but fashionable! The peasant-class stigma began to dissolve with the work of young Malian fashion designer Seydou Nourou Doumbia, also known as Chris Seydou. Designing in Paris in the late 1970s, his unabashed use of mudcloth for clothing and accessories is credited with bringing mudcloth to the forefront of style for apparel and home decor alike.

The continued demand for mudcloth has resulted in simplified local techniques, mass-produced versions, and "mudcloth inspired" looks around the world. In recent years, production of the cloth has been taken up by young Malian men as well as the women, and experimentation has led to less time- and labor-intensive techniques, although the original steps and materials are also still used today.

The lengthy, painstaking process is clearly the most complicated of those presented here. Mudcloth artists spend about two weeks on a cloth, and this is only after the mud has fermented in a clay pot for several months, even up to a year! The base cloth is similar to that used for korhogo painting, with narrow strips of locally-grown, hand-woven cotton sewn together to form a large, rectangular piece.

The entire cloth is first dyed with a solution made of pounded leaves and tree bark. Even though the solution itself is a deep brown, the cloth turns yellow once it is dried in the sun. This first dye serves as the mordant, allowing later applications of mud dyes to penetrate the cloth completely for permanent coloring. The varying recipes of leaves and other materials in these dyes are closely guarded secrets among mudcloth artists.

Meanwhile, the mud dye, rich with iron, has been fermenting, sometimes with the addition of crushed leaves for intensified color. The bogolan artist sections off the cloth, then outlines the designs in mud using a spatula or bamboo sticks. It is the background areas of the design that are then filled in, leaving the motifs a lighter color. Again, it is allowed to sun-dry, then the piece is washed. A second mud application is followed by a soaking in yet another solution of boiled leaves, which helps to deepen the color of the mud even further.

To complete the process, a bleach or caustic soda is skillfully applied to the areas where mud was not painted originally. Optimally, the bleaching process, along with several more days of a final sun-baking, brings back the original off-white color of the cotton, standing out against the mud-dyed background. Finally, the bogolanfini is ready for use as a wrap-around garment.

Try Painted Mudcloth

If you're already exhausted from just *reading* the previous description, consider the following painting technique that approximates the look. The real thing was used for the decorative shield (page 45) and clock (page 93), while an upholstery weight look-alike was used for the pillows (pages 40 and 41). The machine-printed versions of mudcloth widely available today (see the desk blotter, page 96) represent a more simplified version than described above. They imitate the motifs found in authentic mudcloth rather than the technique itself, while offering a wider choice of sizes and colors. These are produced in West Africa as well as other parts of the world.

You'll Need

🏃 *Approx. 1 yard off-white, loosely-woven cotton or cotton canvas (or a large enough piece to complete your intended project)*

🏃 *Acrylic paints**

🏃 *Textile medium to be added to the paints*

🏃 *Small- and medium-sized paintbrushes*

🏃 *Plastic plate or cup for color mixing*

*Black, red, green, yellow, and ivory were used in the project shown

1. Spread out newspapers or a plastic dropcloth to protect your work surface. Plan the symbols and repeats you want to use, choosing from those on page 25, others shown in the book, or your own free-hand designs. (If you're painting a large piece, you might find it helpful to draw out a scaled-down version on paper first.) Also decide which will be the background color and which will be used for the markings or motifs.

2. Using light pencil, draw the markings onto the fabric. Mix paints to the desired color(s), add textile medium according to the manufacturer's directions, then test the colors on a scrap of fabric. Use all of the different brushes to get a feel for how well they cover before you begin the actual piece. Fill in the markings. Brushstrokes should be well-defined, but not overly neat—no rulers needed!

Paint the mudcloth shapes and symbols first

...then fill in the background.

3. Once the markings are all filled in, let dry completely. Mix the color(s) for the background, adding textile medium. Fill in the entire cloth around each motif. You'll probably mix the background paint several times if you're filling in a large area. If you need to mix more paint in the middle of the project, don't worry too much about getting the exact color match every time you mix it; any subtle shading differences will enhance the hand-crafted quality of your piece. Let dry completely.

This design, literally "fighting ground between the iguana and the squirrel," depicts a historic battle between the Bamana (the iguana) and the French (the squirrel) at the Woyowayanko River in Mali. Once the edges are finished, the piece is ready for use as a pillow front, table topper, or wall accent.

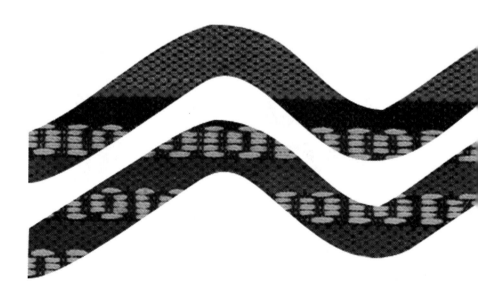

Appliquéd Kuba Cloth

This appliquéd kuba pillow is easy to make. After creating the cloth, follow directions for the Basic Pillow I in Chapter Two (page 40).

The use of raffia fibers for various Kuba textiles is widespread because of its availability, as well as its symbolism that stresses security and continuity. The Kuba people and neighboring cultures of Zaire in central Africa are renowned for their particular styles of appliquéd raffia cloth and the embroidered Kasaï velvet technique on page 30.

Kuba fabrics are widely used in funeral celebrations. The corpse is displayed and buried in fine-quality cloths that are carefully selected and donated by the family. The choice of burial cloths is so important that in life, one is expected to begin collecting special textiles for use at his or her own funeral. The dressing of the corpse is considered to be crucial for proper identification by one's ancestors, again emphasizing the significance of continuity into the next phase of life. Raffia cloths are also associated with wealth, both as figurative status symbols and literally, at times being used as currency.

While the men gather and weave the fibers from raffia palm trees, it is the women who decorate and finish the mat-sized cloths for traditional use as ceremonial wrapped garments, such as dancing skirts. Woven pieces from the loom are joined together to make longer rectangular pieces.

The stiff, woven piece is first hemmed and softened to make it suitable for wearing. To soften it, the maker pounds the cloth in a large wooden mortar. Optional dyes are added to create harmonious, muted shades of clay red, plum, or brown. This softening process is so rigorous that holes often appear in the cloth. It's widely believed that the use of appliqué developed as a decorative means of repairing the cloth, restoring it to full usability. Additional appliqués were then added all over for visual balance.

The use of appliqué in this fashion exemplifies the creative resourcefulness of the textile artists, so much that the beige appliqués were sewn on with dark-color thread around the edges. This transformed the appliqué patches themselves into the main design element against raffia cloth of the same color. Sometimes the pieces used for appliqué are taken from the dyed raffia, for an even bolder visual statement. The relatively simple appliqué shapes are abstract geometrics, with smaller pieces forming "L," "T," boomerang, or comma shapes. Small circles and larger abstract shapes are also used, and the appliqués are sometimes overlapped.

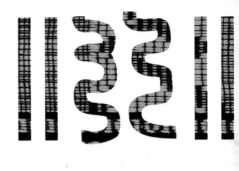

Try Appliquéd Kuba Cloth

A simplified version of this technique involves the use of linen fabric and fusible web (to secure the appliqués so they won't fray). Traditional appliquéd cloths are long, rectangular pieces that can measure up to 9 feet long by 2 feet wide. For home decor, smaller ones are perfect to grace the narrow wall space between doorways (page 49). Smaller pieces can also cover pillow forms, chair arms or backs, or lampshades. Try using one as a table topper, either alone or under glass. The larger ones make stunning wall accents, hung horizontally above a sofa or fireplace.

You'll Need

- *Beige or off-white linen or burlap for the background (select a fairly coarse weave, large enough for your intended project)*
- *Additional linen in the same color or in muted shades of rust, tan, plum, and brown*
- *Trans Web paper-backed fusible web*
- *Contrasting color thread for edgestitching (choose a heavy weight, such as buttonhole twist)*
- *Sewing machine, iron, sharp scissors*

Note: Because you will be sewing through the appliqués as well as fusing them, be sure the fusible web is not a stiff, "heavy-duty" type that can't be sewn through. Trans Web is easy to fuse and sew through.

1. For a more authentic look on a larger project such as a wall hanging, cut the background fabric into several rectangular pieces and sew them back together (Fig. 1). Press each seam to one side. From the right side of the fabric, edgestitch 1/4" from the seam, stitching through the seam allowance underneath to secure it. You can also overlap the edges by 3/8" and sew close to the edges. To hem the piece, press under a narrow 1/4" on all edges, turn under again, and topstitch.

2. Apply Trans Web to the appliqué fabrics according to the manufacturer's directions. Cut shapes from the appliqué fabrics. The shapes are simple to cut free-hand. Peel away the backing paper. Study the sketches on page 29 as a guide, then create your own arrangement. It helps to do the positioning directly on your ironing board, Space Board, or other pressing surface, so you won't have to move the piece once you have an arrangement you like. Try overlapping some of the shapes and position some to cross over any seams you've created in the background fabric.

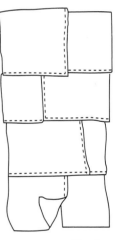

Fig. 1

3. Fuse appliqués into place. Stitch around each shape with contrasting color thread. Try a slight zigzag stitch to add some definition to the stitching. Double needle stitching will also heighten the effect. Try a few variations on test scraps before you begin, experimenting with the stitch selection, thread size, and colors.

Raffia appliqué patches often take the form of "L"s, "T"s, small circles, boomerang shapes, and larger abstract cut-outs, mostly with rounded edges.

Fusing the appliqués simplifies the stitching process, while adding a bit more stability to the finished piece.

Stitching options include double or triple needle stitching, or even one of the heavier utility stitches for a more pronounced look.

Creative Suggestions

1. Tea-dye the background cloth after piecing and hemming it, before the appliqués are added, to give it an antiqued appearance. Boil about 3 quarts of water in a large pan. When boiling, add several tea bags and let brew for a few minutes. Test a small piece of fabric by wetting it first with warm water and then immersing it into the tea bath. Stir for about 30 seconds and check the color intensity. Keep in mind that once the fabric dries, its color will be a bit lighter. When you like the color, wet the entire piece of fabric with warm water and dye it as you did the sample, starting for 30 seconds and stirring continuously to assure fairly even coverage. Rinse the fabric off and let it air-dry. You can speed up the drying with a hair dryer. Press if needed. For deeper coloring, let the piece soak overnight and/or add more tea bags.

Tea-dyeing gives the fabric a faded, more distressed quality that works beautifully for appliquéd raffia projects.

2. Leave the cloth its original color and tea-dye the appliqué fabric to various shades by removing some after 30 seconds, then leaving other pieces in for varied amounts of time. This will give a nice tonal effect to the finished project. Once the fabrics are completely dry and pressed, apply the Trans Web and continue with the above instructions.

Embroidered Kasaï Velvet

Most kuba velvet pieces are conveniently sized for creative use as pillow fronts, wall hangings, table toppers, chair backs, sofa arms, exotic wraps for vases…

While appliquéd cloths were used as apparel, embroidered velvets had a very different role for the Kuba and related peoples. These cloths, rich in pattern and texture, were used instead to decorate the king's court. Pieces were used to cover thrones and as blankets and funerary cloths for the highest-ranking dignitaries. They also held great value as part of one's marriage dowry, upon the installation of chiefs, in presenting newborn babies to the village—much like a receiving blanket—and even as payment for court fines. (This form of currency was later replaced by cowrie shells in the region.)

Kasaï velvets feature distinctive and intricate designs that cover the entire surface of the cloth. The term refers to a textile art made by women in the Kasaï river region. The look is the result of carefully positioned blends of color, line, and texture, so no two adjacent sections carry the same combination, giving the cloth its high visual variations. For example, a wide-lined motif of cut-pile, natural-color raffia would be positioned against thin, black, embroidered lines or maybe red, plain-weave sections to create the greatest possible amount of contrast. The ability to execute this rule of design among the Kuba is an important factor in determining the level of skill of the maker, as well as the overall value of the finished cloth. The linear spaces that separate these sections are referred to as "streets."

The raffia embroidery threads are colored with local plant dyes, creating shades of red, black, plum, and yellow. Strand by strand, raffia thread is pulled down through the plain woven cloth, between a single warp and weft thread, then drawn up again. The thread is then cut close to the surface of the cloth, so two tufts measuring just under 1/8" long remain. This laborious process is repeated until the pattern is filled in. The embroiderer then rubs a blade over the tufted areas to create a shagged, fluffed-out pile.

Amazingly, there are no knots; the tightly woven base cloth is enough to hold the tufting securely in place. On finer-quality velvets, there isn't even a trace of the embroidery stitches from the back of the piece and no real clue as to the visual excitement contained on the other side. Even more amazing is the fact that an experienced embroiderer works through the piece without an overall layout already in her mind, beginning in one corner and designing as she stitches. Most of the basic patterns are taken from a familiar grouping; the creativity lies in the uniqueness of color, line, and texture juxtaposition.

The powerful influence of Kuba textile artists shows up repeatedly in the art of such European artists as Paul Klee, Henri Matisse, and Pablo Picasso. In viewing their works, chances are you've admired the unique aesthetics of African design without even knowing it! In fact, Matisse was so greatly affected by African fabrics that he displayed a sizable collection on the wall of his studio. The international fascination with Kuba raffia fabrics continues today, enjoying mainstream appeal for home decor, both as striking singular accents and when blended with other styles.

Try Kasaï Velvet Embroidery

Consider a cut-pile project that will be handled very little (such as a square sampler of some of the Kuba patterns shown on page 32), safely tucked away in a frame.

You'll Need

🏃 *Loose raffia fibers to weave yourself or 20" x 20" tightly-woven beige linen or cotton canvas*
🏃 *Loose raffia fibers in natural, black, brown, and/or clay red (for cut pile and hand embroidery)*
🏃 *Buttonhole twist or other heavy thread (for machine embroidery)*

Notes:
• If you have some weaving experience and prefer to weave your own raffia fabric, use a plain weave and compact the fibers very tightly.
• For optional fabric tea-dyeing instructions, see page 28.
• If the fabric weave isn't tight enough to keep the tufts in place, secure your efforts at cut-pile work by fusing knit interfacing to the back.

1. Lightly pencil in your design for the cut-pile areas, using some of the designs shown (page 32) and the photos as guides and adding some of your own. Remember to vary the widths and colors of adjacent patterns. Thread an embroidery needle with a strand of raffia fiber. Insert the needle down through the face of the fabric and pull through so about 1/4" remains above the surface of the fabric. Bring the needle back up through the fabric, one thread away from the first thread. With sharp scissors, trim both threads to a scant 1/8" long. Repeat this process until all of your cut-pile areas are filled in.
2. Use machine or hand embroidery to both outline and complement the cut pile designs. For machine embroidering, try some of your machine's heavier stitch patterns, such as darning stitches or one of the decorative options. Once the piece is completed, turn the edges in twice to form a self-binding. Hand sew with raffia fibers or machine stitch.

To form a tuft, the needle is drawn down through the fabric then back up.

Each tuft is cut to a length of a scant 1/8".

Finally, the cut raffia tufts are scraped for further softening of the fibers.

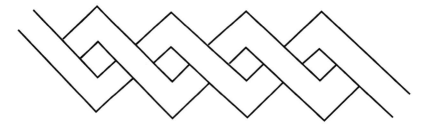

Forest Vines

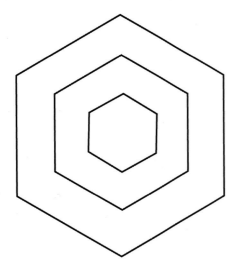

Tortoise

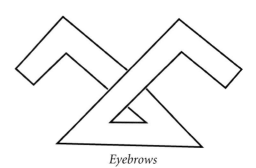

Eyebrows

Basketwork

Kente Strip Weaving

Real woven kente cloth is the most recognized, most colorful, and most imitated of all African fabrics. It is the textile specialty of the Ashanti people in Ghana, its original form dating back to the 12th century. This familiar version was developed in the 17th century, along with Ashanti control of various trade routes; this gave them easy access to richly colored silk fabrics from Europe. Ashanti weavers patiently unraveled these fabrics and sorted the threads, completely reweaving them into sophisticated patterns that reflected the local taste and culture. More recently, rayon and cotton yarns have also been used.

Not to be confused with its mass-produced, machine-printed look-alikes, true kente is woven in narrow strips, measuring about 4" wide. The strips are then sewn together to form large rectangular garments that are worn toga-style. The brilliant colors and time-consuming process involved in making kente cloth connote wealth, authority, and status. Still today, the wearing of kente is reserved only for state occasions and important ceremonies that are sacred or spiritual in nature.

Like the textile arts of many other African cultures, kente offers a wealth of information for those who can interpret the many symbols contained in it. Proverbs, historical incidents, social commentary, and even household items were worked into the kente designs, and several of the patterns are specifically named after renowned individuals, the weavers themselves, or circumstances relating to the use of the finished cloth. When a cloth is completely filled with motifs, it falls under the category of *adweneasa*, meaning "my skills (ideas) are exhausted."

The process of kente strip weaving begins with skeins of thread being wound onto bobbins; this is usually the first duty for a young apprentice to learn. The warp threads run parallel to the ground and extend out in front of the loom for approximately 50 feet. They are tied together at the end and weighted with a large brick or stone to create the proper tension as the weaver works, drawing the weighted end closer to him as the fabric is woven.

(Photo courtesy Barbara Stewart)

Top: Detail of two classic examples of kente cloth to be found at one of my favorite fabric stores, Kaarta Imports in New York City.

Above: A vendor displays one of hundreds of kente cloths available for sale at the National Arts Centre in Accra, Ghana.

Bobbin winding is a primary step in the lengthy creative process.

The loom itself is a double-heddle type, where two sets of pulleys raise and lower the warp threads. The heddles are controlled quickly and rhythmically by the weaver's feet as he simultaneously throws the shuttles of yarn back and forth using both hands. Each newly inserted weft is compacted with a reed (operated by the left hand), giving kente its characteristic tight weave. Yarn shuttle colors are alternated as dictated by the design. All the while, the weaver is working from memory, because instructions are not written down, but handed down orally—and visually. It's a fascinating sight to see! Keep in mind that this is a basic explanation of the process, which can vary greatly depending on the craftsman's level of expertise, loom, and the design being woven.

Once the appropriate number of strips is woven, they are sewn together by hand with a simple overcast stitch, and the fabric is ready for use. There is some use of a broad loom for kente weaving, but it's believed that by weaving individual strips that are then joined together, the cloth's maximum drapability and luxury are achieved. It takes twenty to thirty strips, each measuring about 12 feet in length, to create a typical men's wrapper.

Kente production remains centered in the Ashanti town of Bonwire, the home of master weavers. Traditionally, all designs produced there were presented for the king's approval and personal selections. He would then divide the remaining designs among his court members and other officials. Each royal family adopted a particular design, not unlike the concept of the family crest in Europe. Such elaborate woven designs were in keeping with the overall displays of wealth and opulence of the Ashanti kingdom.

Top and top right: A weaver at work in Bonwire, the world center of kente production. The patterns were learned from the weaver's grandfather and are woven from memory. (Photos courtesy Barbara Stewart)

Above: Another view of the loom, as a textile artist weaves at the Cultural Centre in Kumasi. (Photo courtesy Barbara Stewart)

Try Weaving Kente Motifs

Single kente strips are easy to display as decorative picture frame mats (page 110), hangers for smaller photo frames, or used to border a blanket or quilt design. Although true kente cloth is world-renowned for its technical intricacies as well as its aesthetic appeal, some of its simpler geometric motifs can be interpreted on a basic hand loom. Crafters with some prior hand weaving experience should be able to recreate the patterns at right by studying them.

You'll Need

🏃 *Skeins of silk thread or rayon or cotton embroidery floss in various colors*

🏃 *Fine cotton yarn for the warp (this will show as the background color for the motifs)*

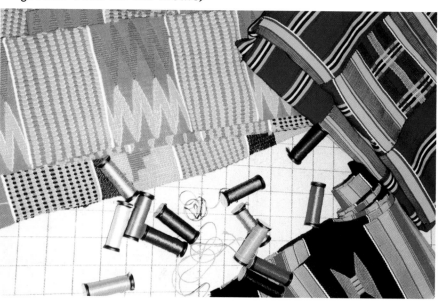

Spools of silk thread like these come in a variety of weights and textures. Alternatives include rayon and cotton embroidery floss.

Set up a warp that is approximately 4" wide. By repeating one pattern or using a combination of the patterns shown, interspersed with design elements like plain and striped areas, you can weave a look similar to true kente strip weaving.

Chapter Two

LIVING AREA

Whether yours is a formal living room, den, or family room, this is your main showcase for decorative self-expression. It's a common area for the family to gather, relax, and entertain guests. Chances are it's also one of the bigger rooms in your home, so some accents should be larger scale to command a bit more attention.

Throw pillows of different shapes and sizes are a basic for any room. Simply change the fabrics to luxurious silks trimmed with African ribbon for the bedroom, or bright geometric kente prints for the kids to enjoy. Here, vibrant designs bring excitement to the neutral sofa.

The korhogo used for the room divider began as the traditional horizontal design, stretched across a wooden frame and simply secured with thumbtacks. After several years as a versatile wall hanging, moved from one room to another over time, it was cut and repieced to fit these vertical dimensions. The coordinating trim fabric defines each separate panel of the room divider and fills out the width.

The rich colors of an authentic woven kente strip give special appeal to a classic arch-shaped clock. It's quick to make and sure to leave an impression in any room. You can make several for gift-giving from a single kente strip.

A second korhogo, complete with rug-like border patterns, becomes a floorcloth in a few easy steps. Notice the less common russet coloring, a blend of Malian red clay dyes that adds warmth to the hardwood flooring.

Smaller accessories, displayed on the mantel, are designed for beauty as well as function, like the matchstick and incense holders. They're covered in distressed craft papers to resemble beaten bark cloth, as is the picture frame. Customize the size and shapes of the picture frame opening to suit a particular photo, treasured greeting card, wedding invitation, travel mementos, dried flowers, or other keepsake. Choose to make it a padded or flat frame, and opt to decorate it with cowrie shells and brass amulets, or simply let a bold fabric design speak for itself.

Kuba fabrics are dramatic enough to simply "exist" in a room, like the Kasaï velvet draped over the wicker table, or the striking panel perfectly sized for a narrow wall space at the entrance. Hanging tabs with button accents and the natural appeal of a tree branch rod complement the woven raffia fabric (page 49).

Projects in this chapter:

⋄ PILLOWS ⋄ KORHOGO ROOM DIVIDER ⋄
⋄ MUDCLOTH SHIELD ⋄ KENTE STRIP CLOCK ⋄
⋄ KORHOGO FLOORCLOTH ⋄
⋄ INCENSE/MATCHSTICK HOLDERS ⋄
⋄ KUBA WALL ACCENT ⋄ PICTURE FRAME ⋄

Surrounded by some of his favorite African accents, Dusty Rhodes enjoys a quiet moment in the artistic yet comfortable atmosphere of his Maryland home.

Easy-to-sew pillows bring color to a neutral setting. From the left: Envelope Pillow, Basic Pillow I, Neckroll Pillow, and Basic Pillow II.

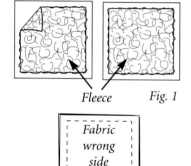

Fleece   Fig. 1

Fabric wrong side 9"

Fig. 2

Note: I add fusible fleece to all of my pillows, regardless of the style or fabric used. It adds just enough body and gives the pillow a smoother finish, whether you stuff it with loose fiberfill or with a pre-made pillow form. I usually include it in the seam allowances as well. Although you don't normally want to add bulk to a seam, the fleece, in this instance, fills out the seam allowance and helps maintain the shape of the pillow.

Basic Pillow I

You'll Need

🏃 1/2 yard African fabric (can be a print, mudcloth, korhogo, kente, kuba, or your own version of these)
🏃 1/2 yard fusible fleece
🏃 16" pillow form
🏃 Optional: Embellishments
🏃 Sewing machine, iron, pins, hand sewing needle, thread

1. Cut two 17-1/2" squares from both the fabric and the fusible fleece. If your fabric print has a particular direction, cut the fabric to maintain a design motif or to center a repeat.

2. Fuse fleece to the wrong side of the fabrics pieces (Fig. 1). With right sides together, pin pillow pieces together. Stitch a 5/8" seam, leaving a 9" opening along the center of the bottom edge for turning (Fig. 2). Trim corners; turn pillow cover right side out and press, also pressing under the open seam allowance. Insert the pillow form, working it into the corners evenly. Slipstitch the pillow opening using small, invisible stitches. If desired, embellish with trims, charms, or buttons.

Basic Pillow II

This is a removable pillow cover with a zipper at the bottom. It can be laundered or dry cleaned, depending on your fabric choice. You'll need the same materials listed above, plus a zipper at least 18" long. For the best results, close the zipper when laundering or dry cleaning.

1. Cut fabrics and fusible fleece as described above. Trim away 1/2" from one side of each fleece piece. Turn under 5/8" on one side of each fabric piece. (If your fabric has a particular direction, the bottom edge is the one to turn under.) Press. Fuse fleece to wrong side of fabric pieces, having the trimmed side of the fleece aligned with the turned edge of the fabric.

2. Pin the zipper to the turned edges, having the folded edges meet, overlapping the zipper teeth, as shown (Fig. 3). Sew the zipper to both fabric pieces. Open the zipper several inches. With the pillow front and back right sides together, sew a 5/8" seam around the remaining three sides (Fig. 4). Backstitch at the zipper ends to reinforce. Turn pillow cover inside out. Press. Insert the pillow form. Embellish as desired, with trims that are washable and/or dry-cleanable.

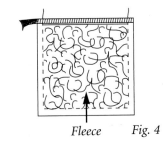

Fabric right side

Fig. 3

Envelope Pillow

You'll Need

- 🏃 *3/4 yard African print fabric*
- 🏃 *18" pillow form*
- 🏃 *3/4 yard fusible fleece*
- 🏃 *2-3/4 yards cording with lip*
- 🏃 *4" tassel*
- 🏃 *Sewing machine, iron, pins, hand sewing needle, thread*

1. Cut two pieces of fabric and two pieces of fusible fleece each measuring 19-1/2" square. Fuse the fleece to wrong sides of the fabrics.

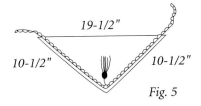

Fleece   *Fig. 4*

2. Cut triangles 19-1/2" x 10-1/2" as shown, two of fabric and one of fusible fleece. Fuse the fleece triangle to the wrong side of one of the fabric triangles. Pin cording along the seam allowances of the two short sides. Baste. Pin tassel in place as shown (Fig. 5). Baste. Sew this piece to the remaining triangle, right sides together, with a 5/8" seam and a zipper foot to stitch as closely to the cording as possible. Turn flap inside out and press (Fig. 6). Baste the long edge closed.

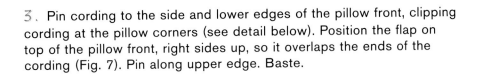

19-1/2"

10-1/2"   10-1/2"

Fig. 5

3. Pin cording to the side and lower edges of the pillow front, clipping cording at the pillow corners (see detail below). Position the flap on top of the pillow front, right sides up, so it overlaps the ends of the cording (Fig. 7). Pin along upper edge. Baste.

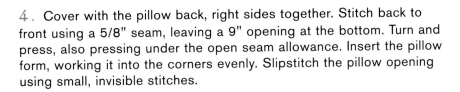

Baste

Fig. 6

4. Cover with the pillow back, right sides together. Stitch back to front using a 5/8" seam, leaving a 9" opening at the bottom. Turn and press, also pressing under the open seam allowance. Insert the pillow form, working it into the corners evenly. Slipstitch the pillow opening using small, invisible stitches.

Fig. 7

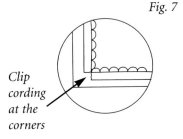

Clip cording at the corners

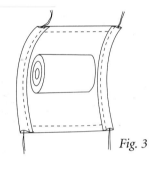

Fleece   *Fig. 1*

Neckroll Pillow

You'll Need

- *5/8 yard mudcloth (authentic, manufactured, or your own version)*
- *1/2 yard fusible fleece*
- *Two 1-yard cuts of cording (raffia, rattail, twisted cording, etc.)*
- *Buttons, beads, or shells*
- *Neckroll pillow form**
- *Optional: Fusible hem tape*
- *Sewing machine, iron, scissors, thread*

*Instead of a purchased neckroll form, creative recyclers can also try unused fabric, rolled up evenly and snugly to measure approximately 18" long x 18" around.

1. For an 18" long neckroll, cut a piece of fabric 20" long x 26" wide. Cut a piece of fusible fleece 18" square. Center the fleece and fuse to the wrong side of the fabric as shown. Turn under 1" on each short side of the fabric, folding it over the fleece (Fig. 1). Hem by machine or use fusible tape.

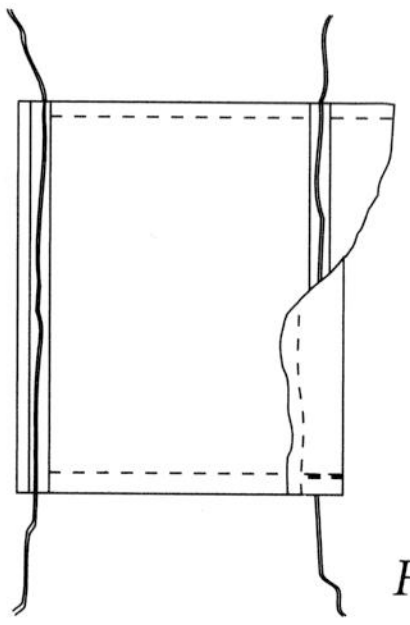

Fig. 2

2. Turn under 1/4" on each of the longer sides. Press. Turn under another 3/4" and press. Open up the 3/4" fold and insert the drawstring cording of your choice, placing it against the fold on each side. Machine stitch along the first 1/4" fold to create the drawstring casing (Fig. 2).

Fig. 3

3. Wrap fabric around the pillow form (Fig. 3). Pin, overlapping the ends if necessary so the fabric wraps snugly around the form. Slipstitch, leaving the ends open 1/2" to allow the drawstrings to move freely. Pull drawstrings and tie. Add buttons, beads, or cowrie shells to the ends of the drawstrings (Fig. 4).

Fig. 4

Korhogo Room Divider

- One korhogo panel, approx. 56" long x 38" wide
- 5" x 8 yards coordinating border fabric (piece the length if necessary)
- 2 yards fusible fleece, 45" wide
- 2 yards backing fabric (can be plain muslin or another print for two-sided versatility)
- 1 yard coordinating braid for top edge
- Six 6-foot x 2" plywood pieces (Four will be used full-length. Have the lumber shop cut six 14" lengths from other pieces, or ask for any available 1 foot x 2" plywood remnant lengths, cut to 14".)
- Three 2" hinge sets
- Four 2" T-brackets
- Eight 1" corner brackets
- Sewing machine, iron, staple gun and staples, screwdriver, scissors, glue gun and sticks, thread

1. Arrange plywood frame pieces as shown, working on the floor (Fig. 1). Join the pieces with corner brackets at the inner corners (Fig. 2). Insert 14" center wood pieces and join them to the frame using the T-brackets (Fig. 3). These will stabilize the divider, preventing shifting and helping it to stand steadily.

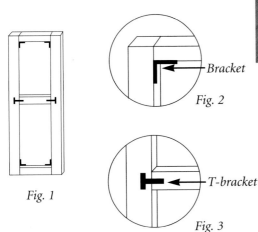

Fig. 1

Bracket

Fig. 2

T-bracket

Fig. 3

The border fabric is actually a stripe section cut from a very colorful print, then pieced as needed for the proper length. Take advantage of the versatility of African prints in this way.

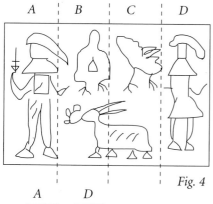

A   B   C   D

Fig. 4

2. Cut the korhogo panel into four strips and rearrange them as shown (Fig. 4 and 5). With right sides together, sew 1/2" seams at the centers to create the two vertical panels. Press seams open. Check the size of each korhogo piece against the plywood frame. Remember that you'll be adding border fabric and that it will be stretched somewhat as you attach it to the frame. If the fabric is too short or too narrow, this is the time for any creative adjustments; add border fabric to the top or bottom if needed. Cut the border fabric into four equal lengths; pin each to one long edge of the korhogo panel, right sides together. Stitch. Press seams toward the border fabric.

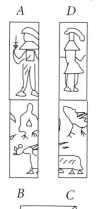

A   D

B   C

Fig. 5

3. Cut two pieces of fusible fleece the same size as the two fabric pieces, less 1" all around to reduce bulk. Fuse fleece to the wrong side of the fabric.

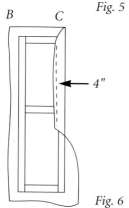

← 4"

Fig. 6

4. Wrap the edge of the fabric over one long side of the frame. Staple it with a staple gun, starting at the center. Place one staple about every 4" (Fig. 6). Now staple the opposite side, pulling the fabric taut and starting at the middle. Continue to staple the top and bottom. Check the overall appearance as you work, pulling gently where needed. The tension should be taut and even, but not tight enough to over-stress or rip the seams! Fold the corners in neatly and staple through all thicknesses. Repeat for the second frame.

5. Cut two pieces of backing fabric the size of the frames plus 1-1/2" all around. Press under 1-5/8" on all edges and position over the back of the frame so the edges fall just inside of the frame's edges, covering the raw edges of the front fabric. Staple in place, with staples approximately 6" apart and even tension throughout (Fig. 7).

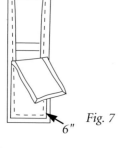

6"   *Fig. 7*

6. Add coordinating trim to the upper edge with a glue gun. For other trim ideas, try a row of beads or cowrie shells across the top.

7. Lay the finished panels side by side. Mark the positions for the hinges, beginning with the middle hinge, which should line up with the middle crossbeam. Place the upper and lower hinges 6" from the finished edges (Fig. 8). Screw the hinges into place.

Fig. 8

Mudcloth Shield

You'll Need

- 🏃 *Approx. 40" long x 20" wide piece of mudcloth*
- 🏃 *Approx. 40" long x 20" wide piece of corrugated cardboard, smooth on both sides (corrugated ribs running lengthwise)*
- 🏃 *Approx. 40" long x 20" wide piece of lining fabric (cotton twill, broadcloth, etc.)*
- 🏃 *3/4" cording (the type used for piping filler, not decorative)*
- 🏃 *3 yards paper-backed fusible web*
- 🏃 *1 yard hanging cord*
- 🏃 *Fabric stiffening spray*
- 🏃 *Glue gun and sticks, craft knife, iron*

1. Based on your fabric design, determine the finished size of your shield. Add 2" all around and cut the mudcloth to these dimensions, into an oval shape with flat ends, as shown Fig. 1. It should be fairly even, but need not be perfectly symmetrical. (For the best effect, choose a section of the mudcloth that complements the shape of the shield, such as diamond shapes or a lengthwise repeat. A smaller, all-over repeat will also work well.) Apply fusible web to the wrong side of the mudcloth, according to the manufacturer's directions.

Fig. 1

2. Cut the cardboard to the finished size of the shield, ending in sharp points. Starting at one end, gently bend the cardboard at 1" increments along the corrugation lines, resulting in a bowed shape. Place fabric right side down on your work surface. Center the cardboard on the fabric with outer edges bowing upwards. Check to be sure that the fabric overlaps the cardboard all around (if it doesn't, trim the cardboard down in size). Fuse the mudcloth to the cardboard. Position the cording along the edge of the cardboard, wrap fabric around both, and hot glue (Fig. 2). As you get to the ends of the shield, cut the cording off, trim it at an angle, and begin again up the second side (Fig. 3). This will reduce bulk at the ends so fabric can be folded into sharp points.

Fig. 2

Lining

Fig. 3

3. Cut the lining fabric to the size of the finished shield. Sew two lengths of hanging cord to the right side of the lining at the ends, as shown. Apply fusible web to wrong side of the lining. Remove the fusible web paper. Turn the raw edges under 1/2" and fuse in place. Place lining, fusible side down, over the back side of the shield and fuse it to the cardboard, covering the mudcloth's raw edges. Hot glue the lining in place at the sides where the hanging cord is attached. If desired, seal the remaining turned edges of the lining with hot glue or fusible tape.

4. Apply fabric stiffening spray to the right side of the shield; let dry completely.

Let mudcloth "speak" to you. One-of-a-kind mudcloth designs should be studied before you settle on a project. Look carefully at the shapes, colors, and repeats on it, and you'll be able to picture the perfect project for it. Turn it in different directions and fold away or block off parts of the design as you study it. When I shopped for mudcloth, I didn't have a project in mind until I saw this particular piece. For me, its bold diamond repeat suggested the shield shown here.

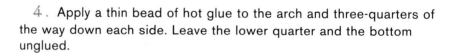

You'll Need

- 10" section of an authentic kente strip (or your own woven version)
- Wooden arch clock, 10" high x 6-1/2" wide
- Clock components and set of numerals*
- Acrylic paints in desired colors
- 3" x 5" piece of remnant lining fabric
- 3" x 5" piece of remnant paper-backed fusible web
- Seam sealant
- Iron, small paintbrush, glue gun and sticks

*Clocks and components are sold side by side, in different sizes, in craft stores. Be sure to choose the right components for the clock face.

The elegant black and gold combination of this painted clock can easily be adapted for a child's room by substituting bright primary paint colors.

1. Paint the clock face as desired. The sample required two coats of black paint, with a gold metallic accent stripe placed in the crease of the moulding and on the ball feet of the clock. Let dry thoroughly.

2. To prepare the kente strip to be cut, first decide where you want the design to lie on the face. Allow enough length for the fringed edge of the kente strip to fall past the bottom of the clock to give the project added dimension. Place a pin through the kente strip horizontally to mark the center of the arch and mark the location of the hole in the clock face lightly in pencil (Fig. 1). Cut away fabric at this drill hole marking. Apply the paper-backed fusible web to the lining fabric, leaving the paper on.

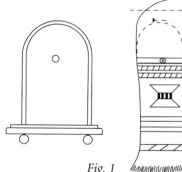

3. Trace the arch of the clock onto the fusible web paper. Cut along this line (Fig. 2). Remove the paper. Line up the arch line with the pin mark. Fuse. Be sure to fuse the cut edge of the lining thoroughly. With sharp scissors or a rotary cutter, cut both layers a scant 1/8" in from the original arch cut in the lining. Immediately after cutting, apply a small amount of seam sealant along the arch line. Let dry thoroughly.

Fig. 1

4. Apply a thin bead of hot glue to the arch and three-quarters of the way down each side. Leave the lower quarter and the bottom unglued.

5. Insert the clock components and assemble according to the manufacturer's directions.

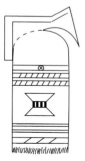

Fig. 2

Korhogo Floorcloth

- 🏃 *Korhogo panel (one with a border design works especially well as a floorcloth)*
- 🏃 *1-1/2 yards woven fusible interfacing, 45" wide**
- 🏃 *Matte fixative fabric spray**
- 🏃 *Cotton canvas#*
- 🏃 *Acrylic paints#*
- 🏃 *Artist's gesso (primer)#*
- 🏃 *Fusible tape*
- 🏃 *Acrylic varnish (sealer)*
- 🏃 *Optional: Non-skid backing*
- 🏃 *Small and medium paintbrushes, sponge paint brush, iron, sewing machine*, thread**

*For use with an authentic korhogo panel
#For use in your own painted design

1. If you are using an authentic korhogo, you'll need to reinforce the loosely-woven cotton by fusing interfacing to it. Cut the interfacing 1" larger than the korhogo all around. Turn under 1" along all sides of the interfacing and fuse edges down. Fuse the interfacing to the wrong side of the korhogo. Stitch around all edges, close to the interfacing's folded edge. Spray the front with a matte fixative spray to help set the natural dyes in preparation for the varnish. Let dry completely and set overnight. When dry, machine stitch from the front, close to the edge of the lining (Fig. 1).

1a. If you are painting your own korhogo for this project, turn under 1" all around the canvas and hem with fusible hem tape. Apply gesso to the right side of the canvas following the manufacturer's directions. Paint your design following the "Try Korhogo Painting" directions on page 18. Let dry completely.

2. Both versions: Apply varnish to the right side of the panel. Varnishes come in matte, satin, or glossy finish. (I prefer the matte finish, followed by the satin, because the glossy gave the floorcloth a shiny "plastic" appearance that took away from the naturalness of the fabric.)

Note: When working with an authentic korhogo, take care in applying the varnish, patting it on evenly with a sponge brush. Gently work out any air bubbles as you go. Avoid a brushstroke motion to prevent the dyes from smearing into the blank background areas. Let the floorcloth dry completely.

Note: If the floorcloth will be used on a bare floor rather than as an accent over carpeting, consider adding non-skid backing (available in home center carpeting departments and hardware stores) to the back of the floorcloth.

The prominent border of this korhogo design makes it especially suitable for a floorcloth.

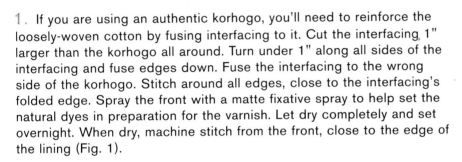

Fig. 1

Incense/Matchstick Holders

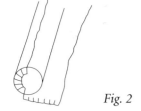

You'll Need

- *13" length of cardboard tubing (check your local fabric store for clean discards and cut to size)*
- *6" x 9" piece of corrugated cardboard, smooth on both sides*
- *Animal print Project Papers (see Supplies and Resources)*
- *Fusible web*
- *Iron, glue gun and sticks*

1. Trace the opening of the tube onto the corrugated cardboard. Cut out two circles this size. Measure around one circle. Cut a strip of corrugated cardboard this length x 1" wide.

2. Hot glue one cardboard circle to the end of the tube. To make the lid, form a ring from the cardboard strip and hot glue it around the edge of the remaining cardboard circle (Fig. 1). If needed, add an extra bead of glue along the inside crease where the two ends of the strip meet. Check the fit of the lid on the tube.

3. To distress the papers, dampen *lightly* with water (a mist bottle works well), then gently ball up and wrinkle the paper. Flatten the paper out partially, so it still maintains most of the wrinkles, and let dry. You can speed the process with a warm, dry iron—no steam. When dry, apply fusible web to the wrong side of the paper.

4. Remove the fusible paper backing. Tear a piece of craft paper large enough to wrap around the tube, with 1" extending at each end. (The distressing of the paper hides any seams or overlaps in the paper, especially when the paper is torn instead of cut, so even odd pieces can be used up easily.) Fuse the paper to the cardboard, using little steam. At the top, tuck the paper inside and fuse as far in as possible using the point of the iron. Hot glue the rest. At the bottom, make cuts into the 1" extension and fold these down over the bottom, fusing each strip as you go around (Fig. 2). Tear a smaller circle from the paper and fuse this over the strips for a neat finish (Fig. 3).

5. Tear a piece of paper large enough to cover the lid, both outside and inside. Fuse it to the outside first and fold to the inside. Trim and clip the paper as needed and fuse into place. If the inner lid isn't completely covered, tear a small circle of paper and fuse or hot glue.

6. Cut a strip of paper 3" long x 1-1/2" wide. Fold in thirds lengthwise, for a strip that is 1/2" x 3". Hot glue one end to the outside of the lid where the cardboard strip ends meet. Hot glue the other end to the tube where the paper ends overlap, about 1" from the top.

7. For the matchstick holder, cut an area of the flint strip from the original matchbox. Hot glue this to the bottom of the matchstick holder for convenience when lighting the fireplace or candles.

Matchsticks for the fireplace and mood-setting incense are stored with style, yet close at hand.

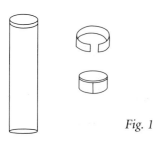

Fig. 1

Fig. 2

Fig. 3

Kuba Wall Accent

You'll Need

- Kuba raffia fabric
- Coordinating fabric for the tabs
- Button accents
- Tree branch
- Optional: Lining fabric (lightweight woven cotton, linen, or rayon fabric) just larger than the size of the kuba
- Hand sewing needles, thread, sewing machine

1. Check the kuba fabric for any areas that might need repair before you hang it, such as loose hand stitching joining two pieces. If the piece is very fragile, line it with a lightweight woven cotton, linen, or rayon fabric. Turn the edges of the lining fabric in and handstitch it to the piece, taking care not to have stitches showing through to the right side.

2. Fold a 10" x 12" piece of tab fabric in half lengthwise, right sides together. Sew a 1/4" seam (Fig. 1). Press seam open; turn to right side and press (Fig. 2). Cut into two* pieces, each 6" long. Fold tabs in half and pin them to top edge of the kuba fabric. Stitch (Fig. 3). Add mask buttons or other accents over the seams. Insert tree branch into tabs and hang, resting the branch onto small nails in the wall at both ends.

*The number of tabs needed will depend on the width of the kuba cloth and how you plan to hang it (horizontally or vertically). A visual rule of thumb is to use one tab every 10" to 12" for verticals with a minimum of two tabs; every 12" to 14" for horizontal placements. Start placing tabs from both ends and work in toward the middle, adjusting spacing as needed.

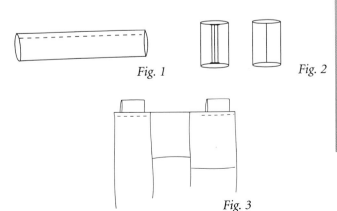

Fig. 1

Fig. 2

Fig. 3

Kuba fabrics can be embellished through appliqué, piecing, embroidery, tie-dye techniques, and cut-pile. This is a purchased Kuba cloth.

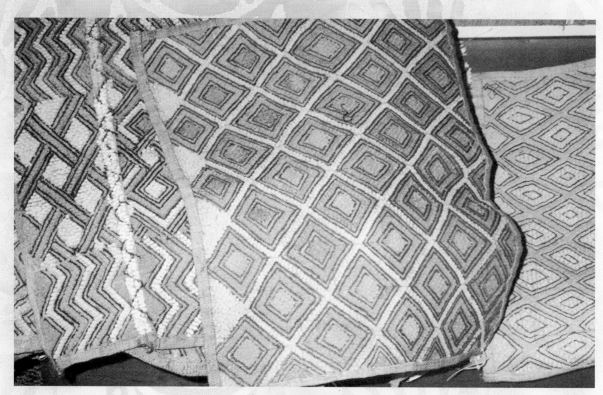

To build your collection of authentic Kuba raffia pieces, browse through African import stores, galleries, museum shops, and some of the online auction services. Note that prices will vary with the age and condition of each cloth, as well as the cut-pile density and the overall complexity of the design.

Other Wall Hanging Ideas

Personally, I love the look of a natural tree branch from which to display a beautiful piece of fabric. I've even collected a few branches in advance, ready for the perfect project. Until then, these twigs of different colors and sizes are stored in an urn, themselves becoming a decorative accent. They seem to fit the mood of the fabric much better than a brass curtain rod. Some other ideas to consider:

• *Sew a rod pocket to the back of the wall hanging, a technique often used for quilts. This allows you to suspend the piece with no visible means of support, which can add to the drama of the presentation. A wood slat extends out of the pocket about 2" to 3" before the edge of the fabric. Picture hanging hooks are attached to the ends of the wooden slat, and all of it is hidden by the edges of the fabric.*

Rod pocket

• *Stretch the textile across a wooden frame and attach it with a staple gun. The frame is simply four pieces of wood joined with L-brackets at the corners. Size the frame so the fabric will stretch to the back of it, giving the front and sides a neat appearance. The edges of the wood can be covered with coordinating trim.*

• *Display smaller fabrics, like Kasaï velvet pieces, in picture frames. Hang square frames diagonally or "on point" for a different effect.*

• *For a casual look, display fabrics using Velcro, or even push pins. Be sure to push the pins between the threads of the weave to avoid damaging or weakening it over time. More delicate fabrics should be reinforced with a piece of fabric behind them where the pins are inserted.*

Highlight a picture frame with buttons. An optional acetate sheet gives your photo an added glossy effect while it protects it.

The picture frame kits by Home Arts include nice quality precut cardboard pieces and full instructions. I use Trans Web fusible web as an alternative to the glue to adhere the fabric (or paper) to the card-board. I find the fusing to be neater, easier, and faster than gluing the fabric, but either method will give you great results.

You'll Need

- 🏃 *1/4 yard fabric (specialty craft papers may also be used)*
- 🏃 *1/2 yard Trans Web**
- 🏃 *Picture frame kit*
- 🏃 *Coordinating trims*
- 🏃 *Optional: Fusible fleece for padded frames*
- 🏃 *Optional: Sheet of clear acetate to protect photo, iron, glue gun and sticks*

*If you prefer the method in the frame kit, refer to its materials list instead
Note: If using Project Paper instead of fabric, refer to the distressing instructions on page 48.

1. Preheat iron to "wool" setting. Cut optional fusible fleece to the size of the frame front (Fig. 1). One or two layers can be used; for a more padded look, fuse the second piece directly on top of the first. Cut away fleece along the inside shape of the frame (Fig. 2).

2. Apply fusible web to the fabric according to the manufacturer's directions. Let cool; do not remove the paper yet. Before cutting fabric pieces, keep in mind the direction of the print design, if any, and whether you plan to use the frame horizontally or vertically. From the fused fabric, cut three rectangles measuring the size of the frame pieces plus 1" all around. Cut another rectangle 1" larger than the size of the easel.

3. To cover the frame front: Peel paper from one fabric piece and trim corners diagonally as shown to reduce bulk at the corners. Cover the front of the piece, wrapping the edges around to the wrong side. Beginning with the long edges, fuse fabric to the cardboard, pulling it firmly and evenly as you fuse using light steam; excessive steam may warp the cardboard frame pieces. Turn in and fuse the shorter ends in the same manner. Cut away fabric from the inside shape, leaving a 1" border of fabric around the inside of the cutout shape. Clip fabric at the corners and along any curves. Be careful not to clip to the very edge of the cardboard, or clipping will be visible from the front. Pull clipped edges through to the wrong side of the frame, fusing as you pull (Fig. 3). Once all of the raw edges are fused into place, press the entire area lightly. Turn over and press from the right side. Let cool.

4. To cover the center and back frame pieces: Peel paper from the fabric pieces. Center the cardboard over the web side of the fabric, trimming corners and fusing edges as you did for the front section. Turn over and briefly press the entire piece for smooth, even fabric application, using light steam.

5. To cover the easel: Peel the paper from the easel fabric. Trim fabric as shown (Fig. 4). Place the easel on top of the fabric's web side. Clip as shown. Turn the lower edges in first, followed by the sides. Leave the top edge of the fabric extending beyond the cardboard. This will be tucked in between the center and back frame pieces.

6. Assemble the pieces as shown with a glue gun (Fig. 5). Line up the easel with the frame back and glue the fabric flap at the top of the easel in place. Be sure that the wrong sides of the center and back sections are facing each other so solid fabric appears through the front cutout and on the back of the frame. Glue the back and center pieces together. Between the center and front, apply a thin bead of glue within 1/4" of the edge on three sides, leaving one side open to insert the photo. For the easel stay, cut a remnant of coordinating ribbon and glue the ends to both the easel and frame back.

7. Decorate the frame with coordinating trims. Cut a piece of clear acetate sheet and insert it into the frame, if desired.

Note: A heart shape is shown here because it illustrates how to work around curves.

Fig. 1

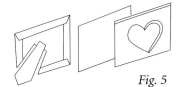

Fig. 2

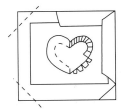

Fig. 3

Clip

Fig. 4

Fig. 5

Chapter Three

VAI:IIN VAI:IIN VAI:IIN VAI:II DINING ROOM

W hether your dining style includes romantic dinners for two, quick and casual meals for an active family, elegant dinner parties, or maybe some of each, it's easy to bring creative excitement and self-expression to the table. Because sharing a meal is also often part of a larger occasion or event, take time to set a table that reflects a look of stylish celebration.

Suggest a more playful meal-time setting with neutral tones of straw and ivory sparked with a red African print.

Formal settings call for a table runner and place mats, enriched with tassels and coordinating napkins. Try these in a vibrant African kente-inspired print to suggest the riches of an Ashanti kingdom.

The fabric flowers of the centerpiece can easily be translated in lighter tones for spring/summer settings, or as shown, in rich red, green, and gold, for a stunning holiday presentation. Wire-edge ribbons make them easy to form. Decorate the lower edge of a triple-wick candle with cut-outs from a favorite African print. Choose the appliqué colors to blend with the rest of the table for an expensive-looking but simple custom touch. For the perfect finish, add adinkra-stamped place cards.

Even the most casual meals can be a feast for the eyes with natural grass fiber place mats, trimmed in a lively African print fabric, and matching napkin ties. A coordinating bread basket completes the look, adding a splash of color to neutral surroundings.

Projects in this chapter:

⋄ TASSELED TABLE RUNNER ⋄
⋄ TASSELED PLACE MATS ⋄ NAPKINS ⋄
⋄ FLORAL CENTERPIECE ⋄
⋄ APPLIQUÉD CANDLE ⋄
⋄ ADINKRA PLACE CARDS ⋄
⋄ CASUAL PLACE MATS AND NAPKIN TIES ⋄
⋄ BREAD BASKET AND LINER ⋄

Deep jewel tones, offset by gold and black, bring unmatched elegance to the dining table.

In most cultures around the world, the act of "breaking bread" together is a symbolic one that signifies respect for and acceptance of those you're eating with. In African cultures, sharing a meal sometimes means eating from the same dish (usually a large serving bowl around which all of the diners sit), an experience I enjoyed at the home of some Senegalese friends several years ago. Although it felt a bit awkward at first, it was exciting to experience the height of communal dining.

Tasseled Table Runner

You'll Need

🏃 African kente print fabric yardage measuring the length of the table plus 1/2 yard
🏃 Lining fabric or second print, same yardage*
🏃 Fusible craft backing, same yardage
🏃 Two large tassels
🏃 Optional: Fusible hem tape
🏃 Iron, sewing machine, two small safety pins, scissors, glue gun and sticks, thread

*Tip: Use a second print to make the runner reversible

1. Cut both fabrics to the desired runner width, plus 1". This might be determined by the design repeat on your fabric or the size of your table. (The runner shown here has a finished width of 13". It was cut at 14" wide.) Cut ends to create points as shown (Fig. 1). Cut fusible craft backing to the same size. Fuse the craft backing to the wrong side of the main fabric according to the manufacturer's directions.

2. With right sides together, pin main fabric to lining fabric. Sew a 1/2" seam, leaving an opening at the center for turning. Trim corners; turn right side out. Press, tucking in the open seam allowance. Close the opening by handsewing or fusing with hem tape.

3. To customize your tassels, fold a small strip of the fabric into thirds lengthwise to hide the raw edges. Hot glue the strip of fabric to the top of the tassel, overlapping the ends of the fabric strip slightly (Fig. 2). Attach the tassels from the underside with small safety pins so they can be removed easily when it's time to launder or dry clean the runner.

Above and right: Line the runner and place mats with a second print for two-sided versatility.

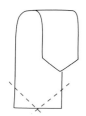

Fig. 1

Fig. 2

Tasseled Place Mats and Napkins

Tasseled Place Mats

You'll Need (for each place mat)

- *19" x 17" African kente print fabric*
- *19" x 17" lining fabric or second print*
- *1/2 yard fusible craft backing*
- *Small tassel*
- *Optional: Fusible hem tape*
- *Scissors, iron, sewing machine, small safety pin, thread*

Cut fabric, lining, and craft backing to create points as shown (Fig. 1). Fuse craft backing to the wrong side of the main fabric according to the manufacturer's directions. To complete the place mats, follow Steps 2 and 3 for the table runner on the previous page.

Fig. 1

Napkins

You'll Need (for each napkin)

- *16" square fabric*
- *Fusible hem tape*
- *Scissors, iron*

Press fabric. Turn under approximately 3/8" on all edges and press (Fig. 2). Cut fusible hem tape in half lengthwise (it usually comes in a 3/4" width). Place fusible tape under the folded edge and fuse. Continue with the other three sides. Turn napkin over to the right side and steam-press again. Complete the look with a simple napkin "ring" of wire-edge ribbon, as shown in the photo.

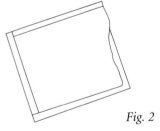

Fig. 2

Note: Fusible hem tape is washable. If the fusible bond loosens when laundered, it probably needed a longer fusing the first time around. You can usually re-fuse it with no problem, because the fusible glue remains on the fabric. Of course, the napkin hem can also be turned under twice and sewn, but fusing gives it a little more body along the edges, which helps keep the napkin's shape for fancy folds, etc.

Floral Centerpiece

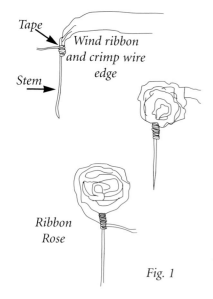

African fabric ribbons with
wire edges are easily sculpted
into flowers and leaves that will
last for seasons.

You'll Need

- African fabric wire-edge ribbon (see Supplies and Resources)
- Green floral stems
- Green floral tape
- Fabric stiffening spray
- Spanish moss
- Floral foam
- Coordinating filler branches
- Small vase or urn
- Optional: Cowrie shells or glass marbles

1. Begin with a piece of wire-edge ribbon at least 1 yard long for the rosette or 1/2 yard for the leaf. You can also work from a spool of ribbon, then cut it when you're satisfied with the size of the flower. Depending on the width of the ribbon and the desired fullness of each flower, you'll need different amounts for each kind.

2. With a piece of floral tape, anchor the end of the ribbon to the a stem. Follow the illustrations for forming the flowers and leaves, crimping the wire to create the shape. Be careful to avoid very sharp creases in the wire, which can weaken and break it—experiment to see just how sharply it can be creased before the breaking point (Figs. 1 and 2).

3. To end a flower, begin winding it down the stem gradually so the thickness tapers off. For wide ribbons, you might want to trim the end of the ribbon diagonally to taper it more easily. Wrap with floral tape. Make any final adjustments to the flower shape by bending and crimping the wire edge. Spray with fabric stiffening spray according to the manufacturer's directions. Let dry thoroughly.

4. Arrange flowers and filler branches. Place floral foam inside of the vase and insert the stems to keep them in place. Cover the foam with Spanish moss so some moss is visible at the top of the vase. For clear vases, try a handful of cowrie shells or glass marbles to keep the flower arrangement in place.

Tape

Wind ribbon
and crimp wire
edge

Stem

Ribbon
Rose

Fig. 1

Ribbon
Leaf

Bend
wire

Fig. 2

Appliquéd Candle

Keep your appliqués toward the lower third of the candle height to enjoy the look as long as possible.

You'll Need

- African print fabric with motifs suitable for appliqué
- 6" x 6" candle
- Glue stick, sharp scissors, pins

1. Cut appliqués from the fabric using sharp scissors. Check the placement of your fabric cut-outs around the candle before you glue them on. It's best to position these along the lower edge of the candle. Be sure the motifs are evenly spaced around the candle for a perfect view from any direction. Stick pins into the appliqués to hold them in place while you arrange your design.

2. Glue appliqués to the candle (a basic glue stick works best). Spread glue evenly and thinly to avoid lumps on the surface of the candle.

One-of-a-kind place cards become a simple but personal keepsake of a special evening. Let carefully chosen adinkra symbols convey a special message.

You'll Need

- Small adinkra stamps*
- Ivory card stock
- Acrylic paints in colors to match your table setting
- X-acto knife or sharp scissors, calligraphy pen (optional)

*To make your own stamps, see page 12, or see Supplies and Resources for the mini rubber stamps used above.

1. Using an X-acto knife or sharp scissors, cut place cards 5" long x 3" wide. Lightly score the center of the card for a folded measurement of 2-1/2" x 3" (Fig. 1).

2. Choose designs for the front of each place card. Refer to general stamping instructions on page 14. Keep in mind the length of the name to be added, planning the designs to run vertically or horizontally as space allows. You can also write the name first, stamping the surrounding areas.

3. Creative Options:
A. Make fancy cuts along the lower front edge or the sides of the card (Fig. 2).
B. Use the space inside for a personal message to each guest, as a small take-home token of the occasion.
C. Select each symbol carefully to reflect something about the guest and share the meanings of each symbol during the meal.

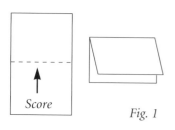

Score

Fig. 1

Fig. 2

Casual Place Mats and Napkin Ties

You'll Need
(for each place mat and napkin tie)

- 14" x 19" piece of woven natural grass fiber (see Supplies and Resources)
- 1/2 yard coordinating border African print fabric
- Button, bead, or other trim
- Fusible hem tape
- Sewing machine, scissors, thread, iron

Casual Place Mats

1. Cut border fabric into 4" wide strips: cut two 12-1/2" lengths and two 21" lengths. Turn under 1/4" on one long side of each strip. Press.

2. Pin the unpressed side of two short strips to the side edges of the place mat, centering them as shown. Sew a 1/2" seam (Fig. 1). Press fabric flat, then fold fabric strip around to the back so the pressed edge meets the stitching. Fuse pressed edge with fusible hem tape or machine stitch close to the fold.

3. Turn under 1/2" on the short ends of the remaining fabric strips. Pin strips to the long sides of the place mat so their edges are aligned with the short sides of the place mat. Sew a 1/2" seam (Fig. 2). Press fabric flat, then fold over the edges as above. Fuse pressed edge with fusible hem tape or machine stitch close to the fold.

Napkin Ties

For each napkin tie, cut a piece of fabric 11" long x 3" wide. Fold in half lengthwise, with right sides together. Sew a 1/4" seam along one short end and the long end, pivoting at the corner. Trim corner; turn right side out and press. Tuck in 1/4" at the other short end and slip-stitch or insert a small piece of fusible tape and hem. At the center of the tie, sew on a button, beads, or other desired trim. Wrap around the napkin and tie. If desired, position utensils on top of the gathered napkin, then tie everything together.

Natural grass fiber fabric is surprisingly easy to work with. The place mats come together in minutes with four simple seams.

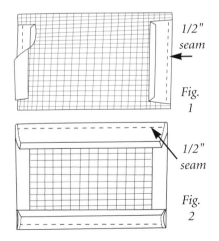

1/2" seam

Fig. 1

1/2" seam

Fig. 2

Bread Basket and Liner

With a change of fabric, this versatile basket style is equally suitable for the powder room, filled with fancy soaps, hand towels, and potpourri.

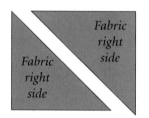

Fig. 1

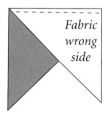

You'll Need

- *1-1/2 yards African print fabric*
- *1 yard craft fleece (1/8" thick), 45" wide*
- *FasTurn tube #6**
- *Optional: Existing basket or container to help shape your basket*
- *Sewing machine, thread, scissors, glue gun and sticks, pins*

*FasTurn is a handy tool that allows you to turn the fabric tube right side out and stuff it with fleece, all in one step. See Supplies and Resources for information.

To make continuous bias tubing:

1. Cut a 27" square piece of fabric. Cut the square diagonally to form two triangles. With right sides together, edges even, stitch a 3/8" seam across the top, as shown (Fig. 1). Press open.

2. Mark cutting lines parallel to the long edges, starting 3" in from one edge (point A) and spacing lines 3" apart (Fig. 2).

3. With right sides facing, bring together short edges so point A meets C and point B meets D (Fig. 3). Stitch a 3/8" seam. This forms a wide fabric tube, offset at each end by 3". Press seam open. Beginning at point A, cut along the lines you drew, rolling the tube around as you cut, until all of the fabric is cut into a single continuous strip, 3" wide. Cut off ends to square them.

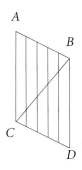

Fig. 2

4. With right sides together, fold strip lengthwise. Sew tube with a 3/8" seam allowance, for a finished tube width of 1-1/8".

To make the bread basket:

5. The FasTurn tube #6 can accommodate approximately 3 yards of fabric tube at a time, so cut your continuous bias tube into pieces for easier handling. Cut eight fleece strips measuring 6" x 36". Roll the long edges of the fleece strip so it fits the FasTurn tube opening. Refer to the FasTurn instructions for filling, turning, and joining the fabric tube sections.

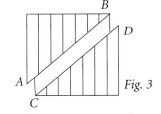

Fig. 3

6. Working on a pinnable surface, begin to coil the fabric tube to create the bottom of the basket. Secure the desired shaping of the basket base by pinning the tube together (Fig. 4). Keep the lengthwise seam turned to the underside or inside of the basket as much as possible as you pin the tube together. Option: Shape your basket around an existing basket, box, or other container.

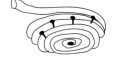

Fig. 4

7. When the base measures approximately 6" x 8", begin to gradually wind the fabric tubing upward and slightly outward. Build up to a height of about 5". When pinning the uppermost layer in place, tie knots at each end for basket handles. After knotting the second side, cut fabric tube, trim away 2" of the fleece, and tuck in the end of the fabric under the knot or taper it off toward the inside of the basket; glue. Starting from the center inside of the basket, apply glue between the coils, pulling the pins out as you go around.

To make the basket liner:

8. Cut two 18" square pieces of fabric. From the fleece, cut four 6" triangles. Baste these to the wrong side of one fabric square (Fig. 5).

Position fleece at fabric's corners

Fig. 5

9. With right sides together, sew fabric squares together (with a 3/8" seam) around all sides, catching in the fleece at each corner and leaving an opening to turn (Fig. 6). Turn right side out. Handstitch the opening. If desired, lightly quilt the corners by hand or machine. Place liner inside the basket, folding the slightly padded corners of the liner in over the bread to keep it warm.

Fig. 6

Chapter Four

BEDROOM

If we consider our homes our castles, then the bedroom is the true inner sanctum, a private place to unwind, restore, and renew ourselves. It's the place where simple little indulgences should be not only welcomed, but expected. Start with some easy-to-make amenities for the vanity or dresser, including a boutique tissue box cover in imported gold batik, overprinted with adinkra symbols, and a hinged double photo frame.

A set of his and hers toiletry bottles is perfect for colognes or your favorite scented massage oils. Male and female figures were cut from fabric and laminated to the colored glass bottles. The Egyptian-themed fabric reflects the culture that was the first to use cosmetics and pampering spa treatments to enhance one's natural beauty and sense of well-being. The crescent-shaped jewel box in royal and gold stripes continues the serene Kemetic mood.

The hat box, a stylish bedroom accessory reminiscent of generations past, gets updated in a regal metallic woven stripe from Senegal. The gold braid design on the lid is an adinkra symbol known as "five tufts," named for a hairstyle that is a symbol of beauty among Ghanaian women.

Basic sheets and pillowcases are revived and made much more inviting with the simple addition of African print borders and matching pillows, while the upholstered bench (a garage sale bargain before the upholstering) keeps a soothing cup of Moroccan mint tea within easy reach.

For a quick and luxurious accent, wrap a silk pillow with authentic African fabric ribbon. The ribbon's wired edge lets you mold and shape the cluster at the center. Secure the arrangement with a few touches of a glue gun under the ribbon cluster.

Projects in this chapter:

⬥ BOUTIQUE TISSUE BOX ⬥
⬥ HINGED DOUBLE PICTURE FRAME ⬥
⬥ HIS AND HERS TOILETRY BOTTLES ⬥
⬥ CRESCENT MOON KEEPSAKE BOX ⬥
⬥ HAT BOX ⬥
⬥ DESIGNER SHEETS AND PILLOWCASES ⬥
⬥ UPHOLSTERED BENCH ⬥

The colors of royalty grace an assortment of vanity pieces. Indulge yourself, or consider these as gifts for others.

For a look of true custom design, seek out trims that blend in with designs in the fabric.

You'll Need*

- At least 17" square piece of firm corrugated cardboard
- 1/2 yard African print fabric
- 3/4 yard coordinating silk ribbon
- 3/4 yard paper-backed fusible web
- Coordinating jewel accent
- Scissors, X-acto knife or razor blade, iron, glue gun and sticks

*The box can easily be hand-cut, or you can use a pre-cut Home Arts kit (see Supplies and Resources).

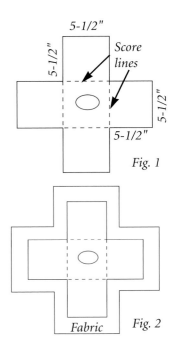

5-1/2"
5-1/2"
Score lines
5-1/2"
5-1/2"

Fig. 1

Fabric   Fig. 2

1. Cut the cardboard to the dimensions shown (Fig. 1), using an X-acto knife or razor blade and a straight edge or ruler. When scoring the top edges, be careful not to cut through the box completely. (If needed, make a few practice scores to get a feel for how deeply to cut when scoring.) Cut the center oval opening as shown.

2. Apply fusible web to the wrong side of the fabric according to the manufacturer's directions. Cut fabric to the shape of the cardboard, plus a 2" border all around as shown (Fig. 2). Peel away the paper backing from the fabric. Center the cardboard over the web side of the fabric. Flip up the four sides of the box one at a time, spot-fusing along the score lines. This will build in the bit of fabric ease you need at the corners when the sides are folded in and glued together. Use a small amount of steam to avoid warping the cardboard.

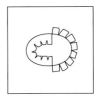

Fig. 3

3. Cut a slit in the fabric for the top opening, clipping every 1/2" as shown. Pull the clipped ends through to the inside of the box and fuse (Fig. 3). Trim the corners of the fabric, leaving about 1/2" extending beyond each corner. Clip into the inner corners as shown (Fig. 4). Turn in the 1/2" edges at the corners first, then turn in the remaining fabric edges and fuse.

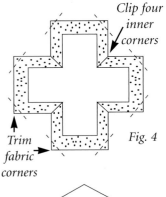

Clip four inner corners

Trim fabric corners   Fig. 4

4. Fold the box sides down and glue from the inside (Fig. 5). Wipe away any glue that seeps through to the outside of the box. Let glue set. Add a decorative jewel to the front of the box and tie a silk ribbon around it with a loose knot at the corner. Insert box of tissues through the bottom.

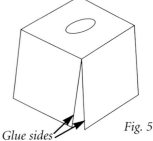

Glue sides   Fig. 5

Hinged Double Picture Frame

Try cutting your own unique shapes for picture frame openings, always leaving a minimum of 1" between the cut-out area and the outer edge of the frame. A width of less than 1" around makes the frame weaker and gives less space to show off the fabric!

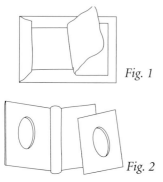

Fig. 1

Fig. 2

To make the basic picture frames, follow the list of materials and Steps 1 through 3 on pages 52 and 53. Because hinged frames will stand without an easel, omit any references to the easel. Instead of the original back with the cut-out section for the easel, the solid center piece of cardboard will become the back for hinged frames. Cut one piece of fabric the size of the center cardboard piece plus 1" all around. Fuse, turning edges in. Cut another piece of fabric, about 1/4" *smaller* than the cardboard piece and fuse this so it covers the cardboard that is still exposed and the raw fabric edges, as shown (Fig. 1). This is the side that will show through the cut-out area on the front of the frame.

To join two or more frames with a fabric hinge: Cut a strip from the remaining web-backed fabric. It should measure the height of the frame plus 2", and 3" in width. Fold in and fuse 1" on each short end, then fold into thirds lengthwise and fuse. Overlap the fabric hinge 1/4" between the front and back of each frame as shown and glue into place (Fig. 2). Continue to glue two more sides on each frame, leaving one side open to insert photos and the optional acetate photo protector sheet.

His and Hers Toiletry Bottles

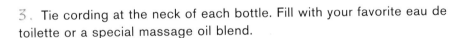

You'll Need

- *Glass craft bottles with corks*
- *Fabric with male and female motifs*
- *Liquid laminate*
- *Matching cording, approx. 12" long*
- *Sharp scissors, small sponge brush*

1. Rinse bottles and let dry thoroughly. Wipe them clean of any watermarks, dust, etc. Cut desired motifs from the fabric using sharp scissors. Check their positioning on the bottles before you begin to laminate.

2. Pour laminate onto the bottle according to the manufacturer's directions. Place appliqués onto the bottle and add more laminate over the fabric. Using a sponge brush, smooth the laminate out over the edges of the fabric, working out any air bubbles with the brush or your finger. Use enough laminate so you avoid brushstroke marks once it dries. The laminate should be crystal clear and applied evenly so it is barely noticeable on the surface of the glass. Let dry completely.

3. Tie cording at the neck of each bottle. Fill with your favorite eau de toilette or a special massage oil blend.

Glass craft bottles come in many shapes and colors, complete with corks. Reserve these special containers for your favorite perfume or scented oil.

You'll Need

- 🏃 3/8 yard gold striped craft paper (see Supplies and Resources)
- 🏃 1 crescent moon cardboard box kit (see Supplies and Resources)
- 🏃 3/8 yard paper-backed fusible web
- 🏃 9" square piece of fusible fleece
- 🏃 Glue gun and sticks, scissors, iron

1. Apply fusible web to the wrong side of the craft paper. Remove the paper backing. Cut fusible fleece to the size and shape of the box lid and the inner box bottom. (Padding the inside bottom of the box gives it a richer look than a regular flat bottom.)

"Gold-leaf" specialty craft paper is the perfect choice to house your favorite treasures and trinkets.

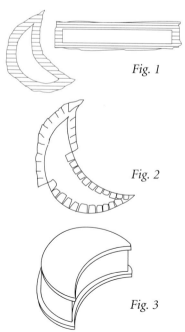

Fig. 1

Fig. 2

Fig. 3

2. Using each cardboard box piece as a pattern, cut these shapes from the craft paper, leaving a 3/4" border all around. Centering the box pieces on the craft paper, fuse paper to both lid pieces, both bottom pieces, and the side bands as shown (Fig. 1). Cover the fleece sides of the outer lid and inner bottom. Turn under the 3/4" edges and fuse, clipping around curved areas as needed (Fig. 2). Avoid clipping too close to the cardboard, because the clipped edges will show on the right side. Fuse clipped edges to the wrong side of each piece.

3. Center the inner lid over the outer lid, wrong sides together, and glue. Center the inner bottom over the outer bottom and glue. Glue the side band to the box bottom, butting it against the inner bottom. Work from the inside of the box so glue won't be visible from the outside. The inner lid should fit snugly when placed on the box (Fig. 3).

Hat Box

You'll Need

- *1 yard metallic woven fabric*
- *1 yard gold cording (1/4" to 3/8" thick)*
- *Plain hat box (purchase or recycle an existing one), approx. 15" in diameter x 9" high*
- *3 yards paper-backed fusible web*
- *Iron, glue gun and sticks, scissors*

1. Apply fusible web to fabric. Measure the box height without the lid and add 2"; measure the circumference and add 1" (Fig. 1). Cut the fabric to these dimensions. Remove fusible paper backing from the fabric and wrap fabric around the box with 1" extending at the top and bottom. Clip around the bottom edge, turn clipped edges in, and fuse down (Fig. 2).

2. Cut another piece of fabric for the box lining, measuring the circumference plus 1" and the height minus 1/2". Position this piece inside the box, aligning the fabric with the bottom of the box and having the top edge overlap the previously fused fabric. Fuse. Cut a circle of fabric 1/4" smaller all around than the bottom of the box. Center this over the raw fabric edges on the outside bottom of the box and fuse.

3. To cover the lid, cut a circle of fabric the size of the top plus 1" all around. Fuse fabric to the top, clipping edges and fusing them down as you did for the bottom of the box (Fig. 3). Cut a strip of fabric measuring the circumference of the lid plus 1" and the height of the lid plus 1/2". Fuse under 1/4" on each long end, then fuse the fabric to the band so the fused edges are even with the edges of the band (the top edge covering the clipped edges of the top fabric) (Fig. 4).

4. To create the "five tufts" design on the lid, cut the cording into five 7" lengths. To prevent the cording from fraying with each cut, place a piece of clear tape at each 7" mark, then cut through the tape and cording. Leave the tape on each end of the cording pieces. Form each piece into a ring and join the ends with a bit of hot glue. Arrange four of the rings as shown in the photo, with the taped edges facing the center. Glue into place. Carefully remove the tape from the fifth ring, gluing ends together. Center the fifth ring over the others and glue.

Hat boxes can be used for much more than millinery. They can provide elegant storage for scarves, gloves, hair accessories, and even keepsake greeting cards.

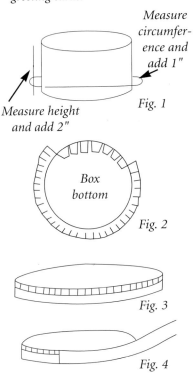

Measure circumference and add 1"

Measure height and add 2"

Fig. 1

Box bottom

Fig. 2

Fig. 3

Fig. 4

An Egyptian-inspired fabric design, imported from Mali, continues the theme of luxury. Refresh your existing sheets and pillowcases, or embellish a newly purchased set. (For the neckroll pillow, follow the directions in Chapter Two, page 42, simply tying the ends with ribbon instead of the drawstring closures.)

You'll Need

- 🏃 *Plain sheet*
- 🏃 *Plain pillowcases*
- 🏃 *2 yards print fabric**
- 🏃 *Optional: Coordinating bias binding for flat piping*
- 🏃 *Sewing machine, thread, scissors*

Twin/Full: 2-1/4 yards x 14" wide
Queen: 2-1/2 yards x 14" wide
King: 3 yards x 14" wide

Note: Because sheets will be laundered regularly, prewash your print fabric at least once before you sew it to the sheet and pillowcases, especially if the sheet and cases have been used and laundered before.

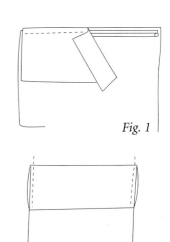

Fig. 1

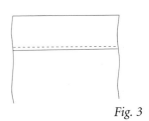

Fig. 2

Sheet

1. Cut the existing top hem from the sheet, cutting away the piping if any. Measure the width of the sheet. Cut print fabric this length plus 1" and 14" wide. Press under 1/2" on one long side.

2. If adding piping trim, cut this the same length as the fabric. Pin piping to the sheet, right sides together, so the finished edge of the piping extends 1/8" to 1/4" beyond the seam allowance, toward the center of the sheet. This will be the visible part of the piping. Baste. Pin the unpressed edge of the fabric trim over the piping, with the raw edges of the fabric and trim the sheet even. Stitch a 1/2" seam (Fig. 1).

3. Fold fabric trim in half lengthwise, right sides together. Stitch the two short ends as shown with a 1/2" seam allowance (Fig. 2). Trim corners; turn and press. From the right side, stitch the lower pressed edge just above the piping (Fig. 3). Press.

Fig. 3

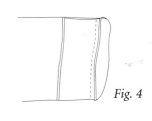

Fig. 4

Pillowcases

1. Cut off the existing hem from each pillowcase, including piping if any. Measure around the pillowcase; cut print fabric to this measurement, plus 1", and 14" wide. With right sides together, sew the short fabric ends together with a 1/2" seam, forming a tube.

2. If adding piping trim, cut a length to fit around the pillowcase. Pin piping to the pillowcase, right sides together, so the finished edge of the piping extends 1/8" to 1/4" beyond the seam allowance. This will be the visible part of the piping. Baste. Pin fabric over the piping, having the raw edges of the fabric and the pillowcase even and matching their seam allowances. Stitch a 1/2" seam (Fig. 4).

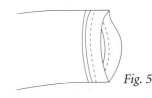

Fig. 5

3. Turn the pressed fabric edge inside to form a self-lining. Pin. Topstitch just along the fabric side of the piping. Press (Fig. 5).

What began as an unwanted discard, rescued for $2 at a neighbor's garage sale, becomes an indispensable, contemporary bedside accent in a matter of minutes.

You'll Need

- 🏃 1 wooden bench, approx. 11" long x 8" wide x 8" high
- 🏃 Approx. 1 yard fabric
- 🏃 Optional: Paint or permanent markers
- 🏃 Staple gun and staples, scissors

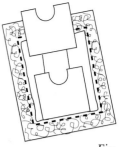

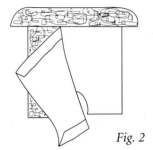

Fig. 1

Fig. 2

Note: In choosing a fabric, pick a home decor weight that is slightly heavier than a basic African cotton print. The best print design is one that will camouflage the staples as much as possible. Mudcloth will also work; just stabilize its loose weave with a woven fusible interfacing first.

1. Study your fabric to determine where you might want to place a particular motif on the bench, such as a stripe along the legs, etc. From the fabric, cut a section large enough to cover the top of the bench and wrap around to the underside. Center any interesting print section or design repeat as desired. Staple along one underside, pull taut over the top and staple the opposite end (Fig. 1).

2. Cut two pieces of fabric the length of the legs plus 1" and wide enough to wrap around the leg plus 1". With the center of the fabric lined up with the outside center of the leg, turn under 1/2" at the top edge and staple close to the edge, covering the raw edges on the underside. Turn under 1/2" at the bottom edge and staple around the base of the leg (Fig. 2). On the inner leg, turn under 1/2" on the long edge and staple down the length of the leg, keeping tension taut and even as you staple. Where necessary, trim, tuck, and staple the fabric to fit around the center crossbeam, if applicable.

3. Cover the crossbeam by cutting fabric the width of the beam plus 1" and long enough to wrap around it plus 1". Turn under 1/2" on all sides and press. Staple one end, covering the raw fabric edges on the underside. Staple the opposite end.

4. If desired, color the staples with paint or permanent markers to blend in with the fabric colors.

Chapter Five

KID'S ROOM

Familiar African cotton prints, with their bright, energetic designs and easy care, are a natural for kids' rooms. With unbridled creativity, young children will love to express themselves by decorating their own space with fun projects like the adinkra sampler pillow. It's a project that combines cultural symbolism and the fun of stamping, whether they choose the potato, sponge, or rubber stamp method. (In addition to home decorating, this technique can also be used for T-shirts, backpacks, and other kiddie classics!)

Combine African prints with other novelty fabrics that have the same bright tones for an eye-catching growth chart kids will love. Let them help in selecting fabrics to create a rainbow effect as shown on page 88, or choose fabrics all within a single color family, maybe one of their favorite colors.

Lovable dolls dressed in authentic-looking ensembles are as much fun to make as they are to play with! (And they're sophisticated enough to display in any other room in the house.) Start with ready-made muslin doll bodies, available in a variety of sizes, shapes, and "skintones."

The miniature flower basket will give any corner a cheerful lift. Instead of foliage, it can also house all of those "pocket treasures" collected throughout the day, from spare change to game pieces and small toys to candy and more.

Not only are African prints perfect for African-inspired projects, but they're equally suited to other creative projects beyond the theme. The bed quilt, an original design by Vandarra Robbins, plays the boldness of printed kente against a white ground for maximum impact.

Likewise, the wall hanging employs a piecing method known as watercolor quilting. This technique is usually associated with soft floral prints that, when viewed from a distance, give the appearance of an Impressionist watercolor painting. Fabrics are cut into 2" squares, sorted into lights, mediums, and darks, then arranged carefully to create the "painting," whether it's abstract or a specific scene or subject. Look at what happens when the calicos, florals, and traditional quilting fabrics are replaced with vibrant African prints! As stunning as they are in full yardage, they take on another life entirely when the designs are dissected for use in quilting and pieced projects.

Projects in this chapter:

◇ ADINKRA PILLOW ◇ DOLLS ◇
◇ KENTE STOOL ◇ MINI KENTE BASKET ◇
◇ AFRICAN WATERCOLOR WALL HANGING ◇
◇ MINI DOLL BED QUILT ◇
◇ GROWTH CHART ◇

A variety of colors and patterns is key for kids' room decor. In addition to the projects in this chapter, try using high-energy African prints with quilting patterns, as shown in this coverlet and patchwork pillow.

Combining fun, creativity, ease, and cultural/educational tie-ins, this version of adinkra stamping makes a perfect family project.

Fig. 1

You'll Need

- *14" flanged pillow cover (see Supplies and Resources)*
- *14" pillow form*
- *Adinkra stamps*
- *Acrylic fabric paints**

*Red, green, metallic gold, white, and black were used and mixed for the pillow shown.

1. Make adinkra stamps as described on page 12. You can choose nine different designs, or repeat just a few of your favorites. Divide the pillow surface into nine equal sections with thin lines of dark brown paint as shown (you can mix red and green to create brown) (Fig. 1).

2. Place a paper bag, plastic, or other protection inside of the pillow cover to prevent paint from seeping to the other side. Stamp designs onto the front, working on a flat surface. Follow the tips and guidelines on page 14.

3. Let the pillow cover dry completely before handling. Insert the form.

Dolls

If you prefer dolls with facial features or expressions added, you can either draw or embroider them on. I feel that the blank faces allow you to use your imagination and make the dolls more versatile. The "Elegant" Doll is shown above, and the "Sassy" Doll is at right.

"Sassy" Doll

You'll Need

- 🏃 12" muslin doll body
- 🏃 1/2 yard African print fabric
- 🏃 1/2 yard matching fabric ribbon
- 🏃 Trims (beads, cowrie shells, fabric ribbon, etc.)
- 🏃 3/4 yard of 4" bullion fringe
- 🏃 Optional: 1 yard coordinating gold fabric ribbon
- 🏃 Optional: Fusible hem tape
- 🏃 Hand sewing needles, thread, iron, glue gun and sticks, scissors

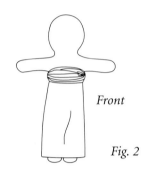

Back

Fig. 1

1. Cut a rectangular piece of fabric the length of the doll's body (from the underarm) plus 1" and width plus 3". Make 1/2" hems (sewn or fused) at the top and bottom edges. Make 1/2" hems at each side (Fig. 1). Wrap fabric around the doll so that the overlapped opening is placed at the side back. Tack the upper overlapping corner with small stitches, catching in the doll body as well. Continue to sew the dress halfway down the length, leaving the lower half open.

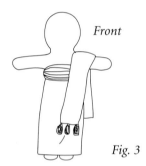

Front

Fig. 2

2. Take a length of coordinating ribbon and fold unevenly lengthwise. Lightly press the folds to make casual creases in it. Wrap ribbon across the top of the dress, around the underarms and to the back of the doll (Fig. 2). Pin the ribbon trim snugly around the doll and sew it to the dress at the back with small stitches.

Front

Fig. 3

3. For the shoulder sash, cut fabric ribbon or a strip of fabric the same length as the dress. (If using cut fabric, make the strip 3" wide. Turn under 1/2" on each long side and hem by machine or fusible tape.) On either version, turn under 1/2" at each short end and hem. Position the sash across one shoulder, angling the ends in toward the center of the body slightly. Sew the sash to the doll at the shoulder and to the dress, using small hand stitches. Sew cowrie shells or beads to the lower front end of the sash (Fig. 3).

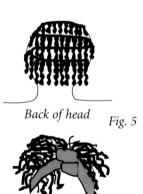

Fig. 4

Back of head   Fig. 5

Front of head   Fig. 6

4. Fold bullion fringe into 4" sections until you reach the desired thickness of "braids" (Fig. 4). Beginning at one side of the head, approximately at ear level, glue the edge of the braid with braids falling toward the back of the head. Fold braid back and continue to glue fringe into place, working up toward the front hairline area (Fig. 5). Tuck in the end of the braid and glue to prevent unraveling. Cut a length of fabric ribbon (or cut fabric 4" wide; fold in about 1" on each long end and press). Wrap fabric from the back, underneath the braids, and wrap up around the head to the front. Tie ends loosely. Arrange braids as desired, coming out from the headwrap, then tighten the headwrap around them. Tuck in the ends of the headwrap; secure with a few handstitches if needed (Fig. 6).

5. Finishing: For earrings, sew beads to the edges of the headwrap at the sides of the head. Add a couple strands of beads across one shoulder; secure these at the upper back with hand stitches or a safety pin.

"Elegant" Doll

You'll Need

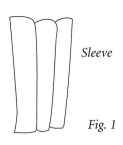

Sleeve

Fig. 1

- 🏃 *15" muslin doll body*
- 🏃 *1/2 yard African print fabric*
- 🏃 *Charm*
- 🏃 *Coordinating fabric ribbon, about 9" long*
- 🏃 *Decorative braid, about 9" long*
- 🏃 *Thin cording, about 7" long*
- 🏃 *Optional: Fusible hem tape*
- 🏃 *Hand sewing needles, thread, iron, scissors*

1. Cut two 5" x 3-1/2" sleeve sections. Turn under 1/4" on each long side and hem with small stitches or use fusible tape. Make pleats in the sleeves as shown (Fig. 1). Pin sleeves to the front and back of the doll, puffing out the pleats of the sleeves, having the ends extend at least 1/2" beyond the underarms at both the front and the back. Sew the ends of the sleeves into place at front and back.

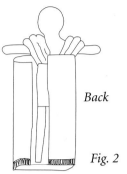

Back

Fig. 2

2. Cut a rectangular piece of fabric the length of the doll's body (from the underarm) plus 1" and the width plus 3". Make 1/2" hems (sewn or fused) at the top and bottom edges. Sew or fuse decorative braid to the bottom hem. Make 1/2" hems at each side. Wrap fabric around the doll snugly, covering the raw edges of the sleeve with the overlapped opening at the back (Fig. 2). Tack the upper overlapping corner with small stitches, catching in the doll body as well. Continue to sew the overlapping edge closed.

Fig. 3

3. Fold coordinating fabric ribbon unevenly lengthwise. Lightly press the folds to make casual creases in it. Wrap ribbon across the top of the dress, around the underarms, and to the back of the doll. Pin the ribbon trim snugly around the doll and sew it to the dress at the back with small stitches.

4. Cut a piece of fabric for the headwrap, measuring approximately 12" x 4". Turn under 1/2" under each long edge and press. Wrap fabric from the back of the head, up around the front, tie, and tuck in one end (Fig. 3). Adjust the remaining end (about 1" long) so it fans out slightly, off to one side of the front.

5. Finishing: Make a small necklace for the doll by stringing a charm onto thin cording; tie the cording. Slip it over the doll's head.

For both dolls: As a precaution, buttons, beads, shells, and other small trims should be omitted on dolls within reach of very small children (age 3 or younger).

You'll Need

- Unfinished wooden stool, approx. 11" long x 8" wide x 8" high
- 1/2 yard woven kente-style fabric (home decor weight)
- Acrylic paints (two colors to coordinate with the fabric)
- 1/2 yard fusible fleece
- Staple gun and staples, iron

1. Paint the legs, crossbeam, and underneath the top of the bench in alternating colors. Paint a second coat. Allow to dry completely.

2. Cut four layers of fusible fleece the size of the stool top. Fuse the first layer to the wood, then each layer on top of the next. To build up the outer edges of the stool, roll up two pieces of 8" wide fusible fleece, tapering them off toward the center as shown (Fig. 1). Glue into place at each end of the stool. Finish with one last layer of fleece, fused across the entire top.

Fig. 1

3. Cut fabric large enough to cover the bench and wrap around to the underside. Turn under and press 1/2" on all edges. Cover the top of the bench and flip it upside down. Starting at the center of one short side, secure the fabric with a staple gun, moving out to the left and right. Staple the opposite side, pulling the fabric taut with even tension as you staple. Fold down the long sides, neatly tucking in the corners. Staple.

In many parts of West Africa, one's stool is among his or her most important personal objects. Regardless of age or social status, the stool is a common cultural possession. They are often given as gifts or to mark special events in one's life, starting at birth. Usually carved from one solid piece of wood, the stool curves upward at the edges and features elaborate carvings in the center. Stools are a favorite item for both novice and experienced collectors of African art. Create this colorful version as a family heirloom.

Mini Kente Basket

You'll Need

- 1/2 yard kente print fabric
- 1/2 yard craft fleece
- 3" square piece of cardboard
- Artificial foliage
- Spanish moss or other floral arrangement filler
- 6" square piece of paper-backed fusible web
- FasTurn tube #5*
- Sewing machine, thread, glue gun and sticks, pins

*FasTurn is a handy tool that allows you to turn the fabric tube right side out and stuff it with fleece, all in one step (see Supplies and Resources).

One of the most popular designs in printed kente was used for this mini basket. Use it any place in the house, wherever you need a small splash of color.

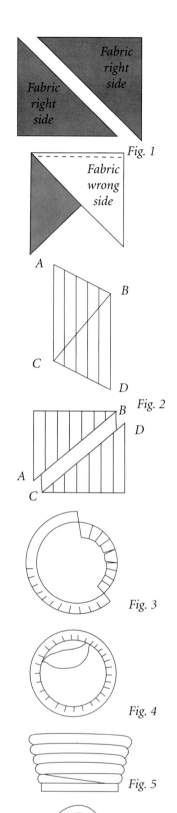

Fabric right side

Fabric right side

Fig. 1

Fabric wrong side

A

B

C

D

Fig. 2

B

D

A

C

Fig. 3

Fig. 4

Fig. 5

Fig. 6

To make the continuous bias tubing:

1. Cut a 16" square piece of fabric. Cut the square diagonally to form two triangles. With right sides together, edges even, stitch a 3/8" seam (Fig. 1). Press open.

2. Mark cutting lines parallel to the long edges, starting 2-1/4" in from one edge (point A) and spacing lines 2-1/4" apart.

3. With right sides facing, bring together short edges so point A meets C and point B meets D (Fig. 2). Stitch a 3/8" seam. This forms a wide fabric tube, offset at each end by 2-1/4". Press seam open. Beginning at point A, cut along the lines you drew, rolling the fabric around as you cut, until all of the fabric is cut into a single continuous strip, 2-1/4" wide. Cut off the ends to square them.

4. With right sides together, fold the strip lengthwise. Sew tube with a 3/8" seam allowance, for a finished tube width of 13/16".

To make the basket:

5. Cut fleece strips measuring 2-1/2" wide. Roll the long edges of the fleece strip in toward the center so it fits the FasTurn tube opening. Refer to the manufacturer's instructions for filling and turning the fabric tube sections.

6. Apply fusible web to a 6" square piece of fabric. Remove the paper. From the fabric, cut a circle measuring 4" in diameter; cut a second circle measuring 2-3/4" in diameter. Cut the corners from the cardboard piece to form a circle. Fuse the 4" fabric to it, clipping the edges and fusing to the edges to the opposite side (Fig. 3). Avoid clipping too close to the cardboard so the clipped edges won't show on the face. Position the smaller fabric circle over the exposed cardboard, covering all of the clippings; fuse (Fig. 4).

7. Cut one end of the filled fabric tube diagonally so it will taper upward gradually. Begin pinning, then gluing, the tube around the edge of the cardboard base. Build up about five to six rounds, then cut the tube at the end opposite of where the tube begins, to make the finished height as even as possible. Again cut the tube at an angle to taper it down, cutting away some of the fleece inside of the fabric tube. Glue the end toward the inside of the basket (Fig. 5).

8. Cut two tube pieces 10" long for the basket handles. Cut away 1/2" of fleece from each end. Glue fabric ends to the inside of the basket as shown (Fig. 6). Stick Spanish moss into the basket and arrange foliage as desired, or use the basket for emptied pockets, small toys, game pieces, etc.

African Watercolor Wall Hanging

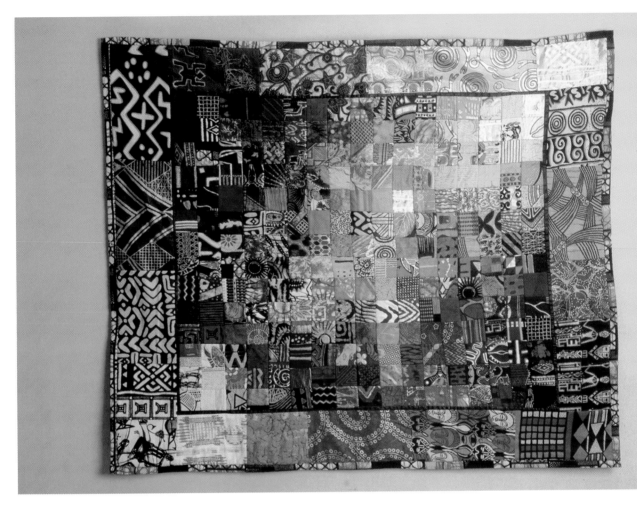

You'll Need (for a finished size approx. 30" x 35")

- 2" fabric squares (need 238)*
- 1-1/2 yard Quilt Fuse 2" fusible grid
- Eighteen to twenty different border fabrics, each approx. 9" square
- 1-1/4 yard backing/binding fabric
- 1 yard low-loft fleece
- 2-1/2 yards black 3/4" bias binding
- Sewing machine, thread, iron

*Note: You don't necessarily need 238 different cotton African print fabrics, although for serious collectors, it's a lofty and worthwhile goal to strive for! Until then, cut different 2" sections from the same print and use both backs and fronts of some fabrics to multiply your print stash. Then, add in some non-African transitional fabrics; some of my favorite textures include silk douppioni, silk tweed, Ultrasuede, batiks, hand-dyed and sueded cottons, plain and novelty linens, as well as a few traditional quilting prints.

African fabrics adapt beautifully to watercolor quilting, a technique that usually employs soft pastel florals and calico prints.

1. Sort all of the fabrics to blend into general color groups, for example: reds → oranges → golds → lime greens → blue-greens → blues → violets and purples then through blacks then browns and back to reds.

2. Place the Quilt Fuse, fusible side up, on a table, Space Board work surface, or other large pressing surface. Starting with any color group in one corner, begin to arrange the fabric squares, blending one color family into another gradually. Place one fabric square in each 2" square on the grid. Build uneven "blocks" of color, rather than arranging them in straight lines. Use the above photo as a general guide. Note that beige areas will naturally form around the center as your transitional fabrics. In this sample, dark and light corners emerged at opposite ends, but your quilt might take a different form.

Fig. 1

3. As you work, stand away from the piece to view it at a distance, making any necessary adjustments in the fabric placement. When you're satisfied with the quilt arrangement, fuse the squares and stitch according to the manufacturer's directions. Sew bias binding to the right sides of the quilt (Fig. 1). Piece together fabrics to form the border. Join the pieced borders to the bias binding, right sides together as shown. Press the entire quilt top.

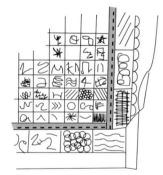

Fig. 2

4. Cut the quilt backing fabric 1" larger than the quilt top all around. Cut fleece the same size as the quilt top. Place the backing on a flat surface, wrong side up, then center the fleece over it, then the quilt top, right side up. Press. Use safety pins to secure the three layers together. Turn in and press 1/2" on the backing. Form the binding by turning in again so the pressed edge folds over the raw edges of the quilt top and fleece (Fig. 2). Pin. Stitch the binding to the quilt using a narrow zigzag stitch or small hand stitches. Add hand or machine quilting if desired.

Mini Doll Bed Quilt

The Mini Doll Bed Quilt is made the same way as the wall hanging, using only twenty-five fabric squares. Make this first as practice for the larger version, or make it afterward with leftover fabric squares.

For added function, consider adding clear vinyl pockets to the growth chart, an adaptation of the Korhogo Bulletin Board in Chapter Six (page 92).

You'll Need

🏃 Twelve to fifteen fabric remnants, each approx. 15" x 7" (mix African prints with colorful ikats, dobbies, batiks, etc.)

🏃 1-1/2 yards of 3-1/2" wide remnant strip manufactured mud-cloth or other border fabric

🏃 1-1/2 yards fusible craft backing or fusible fleece

🏃 1-1/2 yards backing fabric

🏃 60" tape measure (a bright color is best)

🏃 Charms, small figures and masks, buttons, shells, etc.

🏃 Tree branch

🏃 Sewing machine, thread, scissors, glue gun and sticks

1. Steam-press fabrics. Arrange them vertically as desired. Place the bottom fabric right side up, then place the next on top of it, right side down and at an angle as shown (Fig. 1). Sew a 1/2" seam. (Note: These seams are stitched on the bias (diagonal) grain of the fabric. While stitching, be careful not to stretch or pull the fabrics to prevent seams from rippling.) Trim seam to 1/2"; press seam toward the second fabric. Continue adding the remaining fabrics in the same manner until the length measures at least 54" plus an allowance for final trimming and evening of the piece (Fig. 2). With each fabric you add, keep checking the bottom fabric against a straight edge (such as the floor or a gridded surface) to be sure the end result will be straight once the sides are cut and made even.

2. On the back, use a pencil and a straight edge or ruler to mark straight lines down the two long sides (Fig. 3). With right sides together, sew the border fabric strip to the left side with a 1/2" seam. Trim the growth chart to a length of approximately 50".

3. Cut fusible backing or fleece to the size and shape of the growth chart and fuse to the wrong side of it. Cut backing fabric to the same size. With right sides together, sew the back to front with a 1/2" seam, leaving an opening at the bottom for turning. Turn; press. Sew the opening with small hand stitches.

4. Arrange buttons, beads, etc. where desired and sew them on securely. Note: As a precaution, if there are small children (age 3 or younger) in the home, omit these trims. Opt for decorative machine embroidery stitching as an alternative.

5. Hot glue the tape measure along the border fabric, having the 6" mark at the bottom edge of the growth chart. Cut off lower end of the tape measure.

6. To make the two hanging tabs, cut a 4" x 8" piece from two different prints. Cut a 2" x 8" piece of fusible fleece and fuse to one side of each fabric as shown (Fig. 4).

7. Fold fabric lengthwise, right sides together, and sew a 1/4" seam (Fig. 5). Turn; press. Cut strip in half (Fig. 6). Fold each tab in half and sew to the top of the growth chart as shown (Fig. 7). Insert the tree branch through the tabs and rest the branch on two small nails in the wall. Hang the chart so the edge is 6" up from the floor.

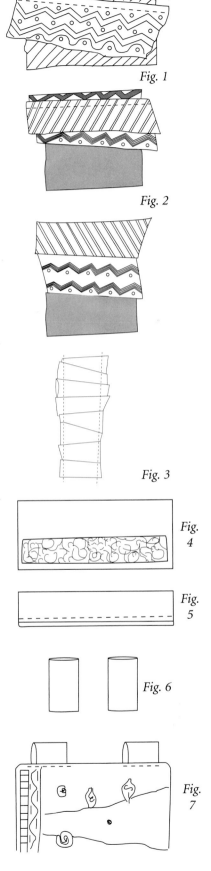

Fig. 1

Fig. 2

Fig. 3

Fig. 4

Fig. 5

Fig. 6

Fig. 7

Chapter Six

HOME OFFICE

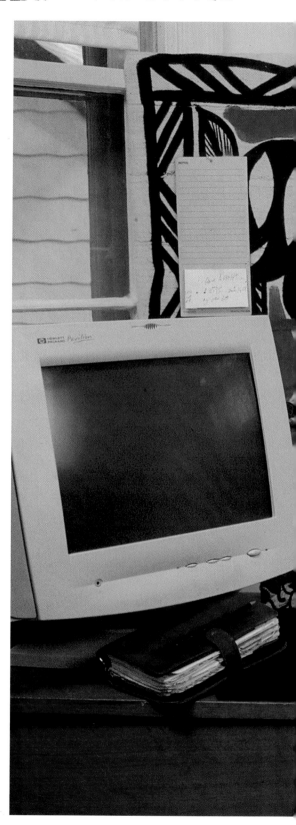

One of the joys of working at home is the absence of corporate restrictions in defining your workspace. It's easy to understand how surrounding yourself with objects that reflect your style can only make you more at peace while you work. Create a home office environment that feeds your creativity, no matter what type of work you do.

Not only are these pieces functional and efficient, they'll also blend in easily with the rest of your decor. As a bonus, you'll find that the earthiness of a few African accents throughout your office helps to take the edge off of the hurried, high-tech pace many of us tend to maintain.

Begin with a commanding korhogo bulletin board, complete with clear vinyl pockets to keep memos and important papers out of the way, but visibly close at hand.

Authentic mudcloth was chosen for the face of the desk clock. Imported machine-made mudcloth is the focal point of the desk blotter, trimmed in luxe black Ultrasuede and protected with clear Plexiglas.

Adinkra stamping graces the lower edge of a simple craft-paper lampshade. You might choose a symbol that somehow relates to your line of work or personal beliefs, or maybe one that simply works with the style of your lamp base, like the popular swirl design of the "ram's horns," a sign of strength.

Projects in this chapter:

⋄ KORHOGO BULLETIN BOARD ⋄
⋄ MUDCLOTH DESK CLOCK ⋄
⋄ ADINKRA LAMP ⋄
⋄ DESK ORGANIZERS ⋄
⋄ DESK BLOTTER ⋄

Create a work atmosphere that is as attractive as it is efficient.

Korhogo Bulletin Board

The korhogo appears again, this time as a stunning two-tone, with the practicality of clear vinyl pockets for quick access to office papers.

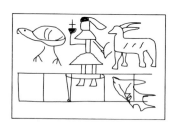

Fig. 1

Fig. 2

You'll Need

- Korhogo panel
- 1/8" thick particle board*
- 1/2" thick foam rubber to cover the board*
- 1-1/2 yards heavy gauge clear vinyl
- 3-1/2 yards of 2" wide fabric trim or bias binding
- Two picture hanging hooks
- Glue gun and sticks, sewing machine, thread, scissors

*An old cork board can be used in place of the particle board and foam rubber if it fits the dimensions of the korhogo panel.

1. The size of the particle board and foam rubber will depend on the size of your korhogo. Cut them to measure 2" smaller than the korhogo on all sides.

2. Cut the clear vinyl 12" long and the crosswise measurement of the korhogo panel minus 8". Bind all sides of the vinyl with fabric trim or bias binding. (Strips of Ultrasuede were used for this sample. Its non-raveling edges made it easy to handle—also, the color just happened to match!) Fold strip in half lengthwise, encasing the plastic, and machine stitch through all layers, close to the edges of the strip (Fig. 1).

3. Plan the placement of the clear pocket along the korhogo. If desired, create some depth in one or two of the pockets by adding 1" pleats at the lower edge of the pocket as shown (Fig. 2).

4. Sew the pocket to the korhogo at the sides and lower edge, stitching across any pleats you've added, and reinforcing stitching at the corners. Divide into various pocket sizes by stitching as shown (Fig. 3).

5. Glue foam rubber to the particle board. Stretch the korhogo over both, wrapping the ends around to the back. Working on the top edge first, use hot glue or a staple gun to secure. Then secure the bottom edge, pulling the korhogo firmly and evenly. Continue with the sides. Attach two picture hanging hooks to the back.

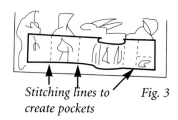

Stitching lines to create pockets   *Fig. 3*

Mudcloth Desk Clock

You'll Need

- 9" square piece of mudcloth
- 9" square piece of plain cotton backing fabric
- Set of clock components (see Supplies and Resources)
- Oval wooden clock plaque (see Supplies and Resources)
- 1/4 yard paper-backed fusible web
- Two large and two small cowrie shells
- Scissors, glue gun and sticks

1. Apply fusible web to the wrong side of the mudcloth. Fuse mudcloth to the face of the wooden plaque. Cut away mudcloth at the drill hole in the clock face (Fig. 1). Turn under edges of the mudcloth; trim fabric to approximately 1" all around and fuse to the back of the clock (Fig. 2).

2. Apply fusible web to the backing fabric. Cut backing fabric to the size of the wooden oval. Turn under a scant 1/4" on all edges of the backing fabric and fuse. Fuse to the back of the clock. Cut away fabric at the center hole of the clock.

3. Insert clock shaft through the hole and complete clock assembly according to the manufacturer's directions. Glue large cowrie shells to the "12" and "6" positions; glue smaller shells to the "3" and "9" positions (Fig. 3). Put in battery and place clock on a photo easel for desk use or hang on the wall.

Shown here on a picture easel for desk use, the clock can also be hung on a wall.

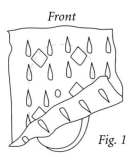

Front

Fig. 1

Back

Fig. 2

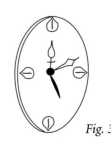

Fig. 3

You'll Need

- Ready-to-decorate paper lampshade
- Coordinating base
- Adinkra stamps* (see Chapter One, page 12)
- Acrylic paints (black and red or your choice of colors)

*For this project, a sponge stamp was used.

1. Choose a desired stamp design from pages 15 to 17. Before actually stamping the lampshade, space out the design along the perimeter of the lampshade. If more spacing is needed in order to end on an even repeat, consider adding a dot, diamond shape, or other accent between each stamped motif, as shown in the sample. Use very light pencil marks to mark the spacing. Mix paints to your desired color.

2. Stamp the design according to the directions on page 14. To add some definition to the shade, paint a 1" border around the top. Let dry completely.

As if made for each other, the "ram's horn" adinkra design echoes the shape of the lamp base.

Desk Organizers

You'll Need

- 🏃 Cardboard boxes*, basswood boxes, and/or Home Arts pencil cup kit
- 🏃 Animal print Project Papers (see Supplies and Resources)
- 🏃 Paper-backed fusible web
- 🏃 Optional: Twigs, oversized buttons, brass accents, shells, beads, fabric ribbon, etc.
- 🏃 Iron, glue gun and sticks or glue stick (optional)

*If you save small cardboard boxes from gifts or purchased items and can't bring yourself to throw them away because they're still like new and begging to be recycled creatively, pull them out now; this is the perfect project for them.

1. To distress the craft papers, dampen *lightly* with water (a mist bottle works well), then gently ball up and wrinkle the paper. Flatten the paper out partially, so it still maintains most of the wrinkles, and let dry. You can speed the process with a warm, dry iron—no steam. When dry, apply fusible web to the paper.

2. Remove fusible paper backing. Tear a piece of paper large enough to cover the most visible surfaces of the container, with enough to wrap around to the bottom. Tear paper where needed to make it conform to the shape of your container. The distressing of the paper hides any seams or overlaps in the paper, especially when the paper is torn instead of cut, so even odd-shaped paper pieces can be used up easily. Fuse paper to box, using little steam. Cover the bottom of the box. Cover the inside if desired, using a glue gun or glue stick where you are unable to fuse. Cover the box lid in the same manner, first covering the most visible part, then the inside.

3. Desk organizers can be decorated with twigs, oversized buttons, brass accents, shells, beads, fabric ribbon, etc.

The trio of desk organizers is covered in distressed African-inspired craft paper. The muted colors and wrinkled texture give them the effect of beaten bark cloth, an ancient fiber art that was popular in sub-Saharan Africa. As the name implies, bundled fibers from tree barks would be pounded into a felt-like textile. The nonwoven fabric could then be pieced, embroidered, dyed, painted, or appliquéd for use as floor mats, blankets, and wrapper-style garments. As more durable cotton yarns became available and weaving techniques developed in the region, the use of beaten bark cloth decreased.

Desk Blotter

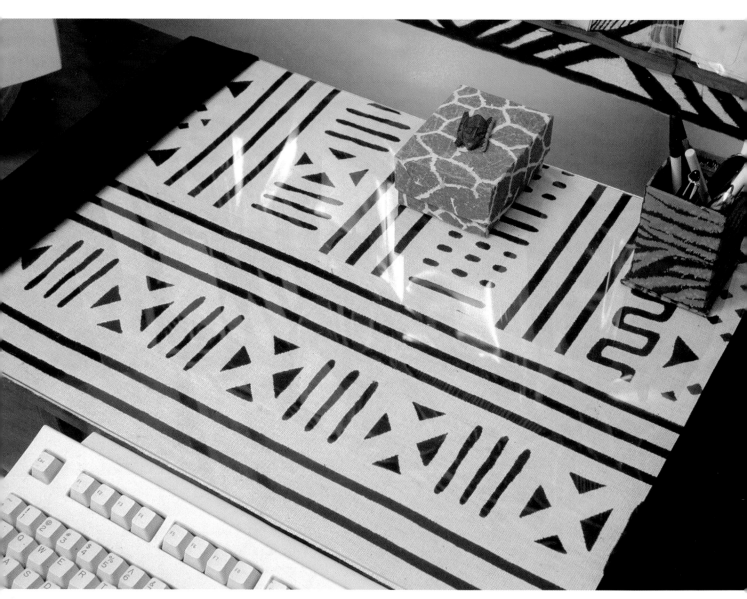

Manufactured mudcloth was cut in the center and repieced so that lines could appear both vertically and horizontally for added visual interest.

You'll Need

- 33" x 22" wide long woven mudcloth
- 29" x 18" wide long piece of 1/8" thick particle board
- 24" x 18" wide long piece of 1/8" thick Plexiglas (standard pre-cut size)
- 24" x 22" wide long piece of side band fabric*
- 18" x 16" wide long piece of fusible fleece
- Fusible hem tape
- Scissors, glue gun and sticks

*Ultrasuede was chosen for the sample. In addition to its rich look and feel, it doubles perfectly as a build-in mouse pad.

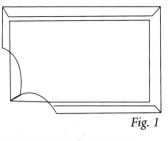

Fig. 1

1. Steam-press mudcloth. Turn under 1" on the two long sides and hem with fusible tape. Wrap mudcloth around the particle board, centering the board so a 1" fabric border remains. Fold fabric ends over the board and secure with hot glue or fusible hem tape (Fig. 1).

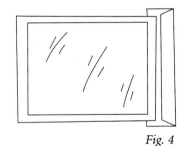

Glue Plexiglas edges

Fig. 2

2. Center Plexiglas across the width of the fabric-covered side of the board. Hot-glue the short sides of the Plexiglas to the fabric, keeping the glue within 1/2" from the end of the Plexiglas (Fig. 2).

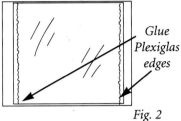

Fig. 3

3. Cut the side band fabric in half, for two pieces measuring 22" long x 12" long. Cut the fusible fleece into four strips, each measuring 18" long x 4" wide. Fuse the fleece to the wrong side of the band fabric pieces as shown (Fig. 3). Fold band, layering the fleece strips.

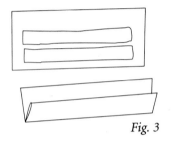

Fig. 4

4. Position the one-third of the band without the fleece under the blotter so 2" extend at the top and bottom. Glue. Flip the padded part of the band over so it overlaps the Plexiglas approximately 1" (Fig. 4). Glue padded band to the fabric, but not to the Plexiglas, so memos can be tucked in under the band. Fold the 2" ends at the top and bottom to the back (Fig. 5). Pull the ends taut and glue.

Fig. 5

Chapter Seven

ENTERTAINING AND GIFT-GIVING

Entertaining at home gives you the perfect opportunity for that extra added dose of self expression. The projects in this chapter work for the host who wants to do something special for guests, as well as gift items for the guests to bring along.

An abbreviated version of the bread basket on page 62, this basket is just right for fresh fruit.

Toast an intimate special occasion with refreshments served on a kente print tray with coordinating cocktail napkins. A fabric tube serving bowl completes the setting. The velvet-lined bottle sack is made with an intricately-woven metallic Senegalese fabric and trimmed with a hand-stamped keepsake gift tag.

For larger gatherings, make a keepsake tasseled guest book that circulates during the party, with each guest writing a special sentiment for the occasion. Pick a fabric with gold accents to match the mood of the big event, whether it's a wedding, shower, baby-naming ceremony, anniversary, or holiday party.

Even a casual game of spades, bid whist, or pokeno takes on a bit of visual excitement with playing cards stored in their own fabric-covered caddy. Choose a wooden box with enough room to hold scorepads and pens, too.

When giving gifts, it's the thought that counts, and the thought means even more when accompanied by one-of-a-kind greeting cards and special wrappings. They'll be treasured almost as much as the gift inside! The drawstring pouch and corrugated gift box can even be re-used and enjoyed among family members, while the fabric ribbon mini-basket is the perfect container for party favors or small gifts.

Projects in this chapter:

◇ KENTE PRINT SERVING TRAY ◇
◇ COCKTAIL NAPKINS ◇ WINE SACK ◇
◇ GUEST BOOK AND BOOKMARK ◇
◇ PLAYING CARD CADDY ◇
◇ GREETING CARDS AND GIFT TAGS ◇
◇ DRAWSTRING POUCH ◇
◇ FABRIC RIBBON BASKET ◇
◇ CORRUGATED GIFT BOX ◇

Make guests feel special with fabric cocktail napkins done in a rich gold metallic African mask print. If you're the guest, impress your host or hostess with a great vintage presented in a velvet-lined wine sack.

Set the tone for casual elegance with a brilliantly colored kente serving tray, then add coordinating pieces from this chapter. Serve your friends in style, or create the entire grouping as an unforgettable gift.

You'll Need

- 11" x 14" clear Lucite box picture frame
- Kente print fabric, at least 12" x 15"
- Fabric laminate
- Sharp scissors or rotary cutter, sponge brush, iron

1. Steam-press fabric. Cut fabric to the size of the outside of the Lucite frame. Use a sharp scissors or rotary cutter to assure a clean, straight cut.

2. Apply fabric laminate to the back of the frame, following the manufacturer's directions. Position the fabric onto the frame. Add more laminate over the fabric until it is saturated. Smooth with your finger or a sponge brush, working out any air bubbles. Let sit, fabric side up, until completely dry. The inside of the tray can be wiped clean; washing the tray in water will loosen the fabric.

Cocktail Napkins

Easy yet stylish, fabric cocktail napkins also make a great gift for the guest to give to a favorite host or hostess.

You'll Need (for each napkin)

- 8-1/2" square piece of fabric
- 1/2 yard fusible hem tape
- Iron

Steam-press fabric. Turn under approximately 3/8" on all sides and press. Cut fusible hem tape in half lengthwise (it usually comes in a 3/4" width), then fold each strip in half and cut, for four pieces measuring 9" long x 3/8" wide. Place fusible tape under one folded fabric edge and fuse. Continue with the other three sides. Turn the napkin over to the right side and steam-press again.

Note: Fusible hem tape is washable. If the fusible bond loosens when laundered, it probably needed a longer fusing the first time around. You can usually re-fuse it with no problem, because the fusible glue remains on the fabric. Of course, the napkin hem can also be turned under twice and sewn, but fusing gives it a little more body along the edges, which helps keep the napkin's shape for fancy folds, etc.

You'll Need

- *3/8 yard woven African fabric*
- *1/4 yard coordinating fabric (velvet was used in this sample)*
- *1-1/2 yards of 1/8" thick gold cording*
- *Sewing machine, scissors, hole punch, thread*

1. Cut the sack fabric 12" long x 13" wide. (If there is a print area you want to highlight, be sure this is at the center of the cut fabric piece.) Cut the upper coordinating fabric 8" long x 13" wide. Press under 1/4" at the top of the upper fabric. Sew the two pieces, right sides together, with a 1/2" seam as shown (Fig. 1). Press seam open. Bring lengthwise edges together, right sides in again, and sew a 1/2" seam (Fig. 2). Press seam open. Fold down half of the upper fabric, forming a self-lining (Fig. 3). Slipstitch the pressed 1/4" edge in place along the seamline. Press.

Fig. 1   Fig. 2   Fig. 3

2. With the sack still inside out, flatten the sack and reposition it so the lengthwise seam is centered. This will be the back of the sack. Stitch a 1/2" seam at the bottom (Fig. 4). Press seam open. Pin or mark 1-1/2" in from each corner. Sew across at this point on each side to create depth (Fig. 5).

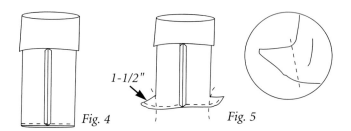

Fig. 4   1-1/2"   Fig. 5

Create this elegant wine sack as a family treasure to share back and forth with each special occasion. Collect the gift tags as a mini family diary.

3. Fold cording in half. Mark the center of the doubled cording and pin it to the back where the lengthwise and crosswise seams meet. Sew cording at the back using a zigzag stitch. Tie the cording around the sack and tie in the front. Slip gift tag onto one end of the cording (see page 106 for gift tag directions). Tie knots in the ends of the cording.

Guest Book and Bookmark

The simple technique for this keepsake guest book and bookmark can also be used to create a private journal, address book, or photo album.

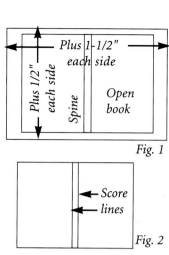

Fig. 1

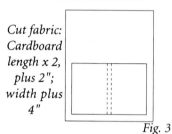

Fig. 2

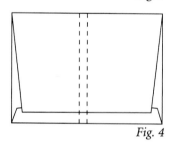

Fig. 3

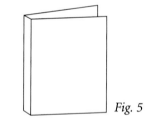

Fig. 4

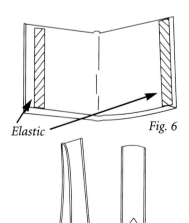

Fig. 5

Elastic

Fig. 6

Fig. 7

🏃 *1/2 yard African print fabric*
🏃 *1 yard coordinating wire-edge fabric ribbon*
🏃 *1 yard paper-backed fusible web*
🏃 *3/8 yard fusible fleece*
🏃 *3/4 yard of 1-1/2" to 2" wide black elastic*
🏃 *Approx. 12" x 20" piece of sticky-backed mounting board*
🏃 *Blank notebook or journal, approx. 9" long x 8" wide*
🏃 *Iron, glue gun and sticks, scissors*

Guest Book

1. Open the book in the middle, on top of the mounting board. Cut the board to the dimensions shown (Fig. 1). Measure the spine of the book. Add 3/8" to this measurement. This is the amount to allow at the center of the board for scoring. Score the sticky side of the board (Fig. 2). (For example, if the spine of the book is 3/4", add 3/8" for a total of 1-1/8". Place two score lines 1-1/8" apart at the middle of the board.) After measuring, put the book aside.

2. Cut fusible fleece to the size of the board. Remove the paper backing from the board and press the *non-fusible* side of the fleece to the scored side of the board.

3. Apply fusible web to the fabric. Place the board, with the fleece side down, over the wrong side of the fabric and cut fabric as shown (Fig. 3). Wrap fabric around at the sides and fuse lightly. Wrap fabric around the top and bottom of the board so the ends overlap on the inside, about 1/2" from the bottom edge (Fig. 4). Fold the piece to check for enough fabric ease at the score lines. Lightly fuse the outer front, back, and spine while folded (Fig. 5). Open the board and fuse fabric on the inside.

4. Apply fusible web to the fabric ribbon. Cut ribbon the length of the front cover plus 3". Center and fuse the ribbon to the front, folding in 1-1/2" at the top and bottom. Fuse the ends to the inside. Cut two pieces of elastic the length of the cover plus 2". Turn under 1-1/4" at the ends and glue elastic to the inside as shown (Fig. 6). Slip the covers of the book under the elastic bands.

Bookmark

1. Cut a length of ribbon 18" long. Apply fusible web to the ribbon; remove paper backing. Fold in half, wrong sides together, and fuse. Be careful not to crease the wire completely, but leave the fold slightly rounded to avoid weakening it. Cut tails into the bottom of the bookmark, as shown (Fig. 7).

Playing Card Caddy

The playing card caddy keeps a deck handy for impromptu games and regularly scheduled card game get-togethers as well.

You'll Need

- Unfinished wooden box, approx. 6" long x 4" wide x 4" high
- 1/2 yard African print fabric
- Approx. 6" x 9" piece of fusible fleece
- 3/4 yard paper-backed fusible web
- Iron

1. Apply fusible web to fabric. Unscrew or carefully remove the small hinges joining the lid to the box. Cut a piece of fabric large enough to cover the lid and wrap around to the inside. Fuse, clipping fabric and trimming at the corners so it lies flat.

2. Cut another piece, large enough to wrap around the sides of the box, wrapping around to the inside and the bottom. Fuse, clipping corners and trimming where needed.

3. To make the padded liner, measure the inside width of the box, then the inside length, from the front of the lid, down the back of the box, and up to the front of the box. Cut fusible fleece to this measurement. Cut fabric to this size, plus 2" all around. Fuse fabric to fleece, wrapping the 2" hems to the back. Glue hems in place. Replace the lid and insert screws or nails. Glue liner along the top of the lid and the lower inside front of the box.

Greeting Cards and Gift Tags

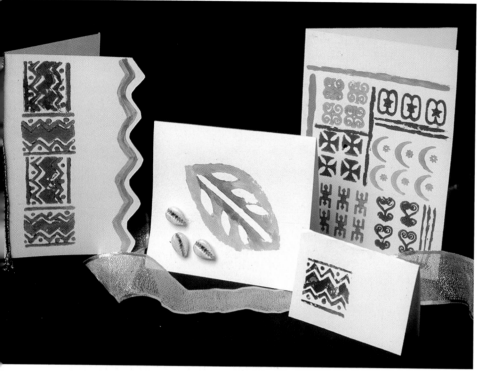

You'll Need

- *Blank card stock*
- *Adinkra stamps or rubber stamps (see Resources or directions in Chapter One, page 12)*
- *Acrylic paints (primary colors, black, and metallics)*
- *Optional (for gift tag): Gold cording*
- *Hole punch*

1. Select designs for each card; make them personal by matching the occasion or recipient with the meaning of the adinkra symbol where possible (see pages 15 to 17).

Handcrafted greeting cards and gift wrap are the newest creative frontiers for self-expression.

2. When mixing colors for stamping, don't over-mix the paints. Instead, blend them lightly for a mottled, antiqued effect, especially when adding shades of gold metallics. Also, try creating a color you like, using it for a few stamps, then gradually changing the color as you do more stamping, like the mini-stamped card in shades of green and aqua.

3. Do a few practice stamps on clean card stock to check color and stamping quality. By using clean card stock, practice stampings that come out right the first time can be cut directly into gift tags.

4. Customize the card further with creative edge cutting and hand-painting, decorative beads, shells, and other trims if desired.

5. To make a gift tag, punch a hold in the upper left-hand corner. Add a thin gold cording tie.

Drawstring Pouch

You'll Need

- 1/4 yard fabric (one with body, such as a woven kente strip or velvet)
- Coordinating African fabric ribbon rosette
- Cording (rattail, rayon cording, etc.)
- Sewing machine, thread

1. Determine the finished pouch size by measuring what will go inside of it. Cut fabric to measure double the finished width plus 1" and finished length plus 3-1/2" to allow for the casing and header.

2. Depending on the type of decoration (such as the rosette shown) you choose, you'll want to add it now, before stitching the seams. Be sure to position your design so it will be centered when the pouch is completed (Fig. 1).

3. With right sides together, stitch the lengthwise seam, using a 1/2" seam allowance, and leaving a 1/2" break in the stitching, 3" down from the top edge as show. Press seam open. The lengthwise seam can be positioned either at the side of the pouch or centered at the back, as shown (Fig. 2). Stitch the bottom edge, using a 1/2" seam allowance.

4. Make the casing by turning under 3" at the top of the pouch and stitching close to the raw edge. Stitch again about 3/4" above the casing, all of the way around (Fig. 3). Insert cording through the casing opening and tie knots in each end of the cording. Once you place the gift inside, add tissue paper or a small cut of garland for a more festive look and tie drawstring loosely.

Africa fabric ribbon complements this rich paisley velvet pouch. Look for similarity in colors when combining African fabrics and trims with others.

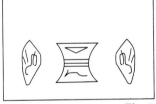

Fig. 1

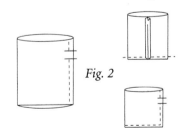

Fig. 2

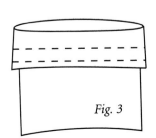

Fig. 3

Fabric Ribbon Basket

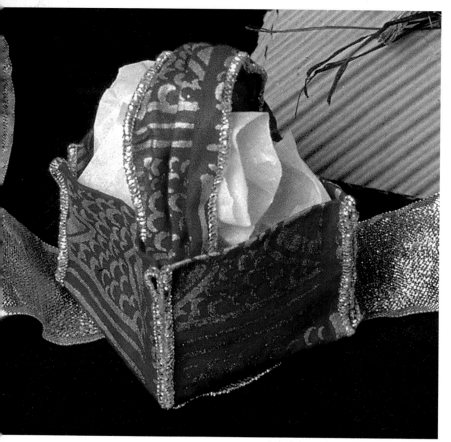

Try these baskets for holding party favors or small, special gifts.

You'll Need

- 2-1/4 yards of 2" wide wire-edge African fabric ribbon
- 1/4 yard fusible craft backing
- Iron, scissors, glue gun and sticks

1. Cut four 16" lengths of ribbon. Cut two pieces of fusible backing, 16" long x 1-3/4" wide. Position fusible craft backing strips over the wrong side of two ribbon pieces so they don't extend past the ribbon edges. Fuse. With wrong sides together, glue one fused ribbon to one unfused ribbon along the long sides, just inside of the wire edges.

2. Fold in 1" on each end. Be careful not to completely crease the wire to avoid breaking it; instead, leave a small curve in the wire where the fabric folds, as shown (Fig. 1). Then fold the ends in to meet at the center of the ribbon, folding wire gently. Turn up 2" on both sides, forming a "U" shape (Fig. 2). Repeat for the second ribbon section. Place one ribbon inside of the other to create a box (Fig. 3). Glue the bottoms together. Use a small amount of hot glue up the sides.

3. For the basket handle, cut a 6" length of ribbon. Form lengthwise pleats and press. Bring the ends together as shown and hot-glue inside one corner of the basket (Fig. 4). Hot glue the other end to the diagonal opposite side of the basket. Stuff with tissue paper or confetti before placing the gift or favor inside.

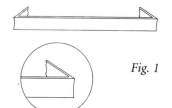

Fig. 1

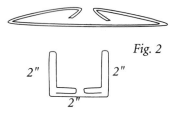

Fig. 2

2" 2"
2"

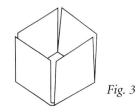

Fig. 3

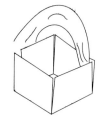

Fig. 4

Corrugated Gift Box

You'll Need

- 10" square piece of corrugated cardboard (or size large enough to accommodate the gift)
- Loose raffia fibers
- Small twigs
- African beads
- Coordinating ribbon
- Coordinating tissue paper
- Glue gun and sticks, X-acto knife

1. Make light diagonal score lines on the corrugated side of the cardboard as shown (Fig. 1). Gently crumple tissue paper and place it in the center of the score lines. Wrap the gift in a separate tissue sheet and place in the center. Fold in the four triangular sides. Secure with a small piece of clear tape. From remaining cardboard, cut a circle about 1" in diameter.

The decorative arrangement on this package is assembled as one piece, so it can be reused or saved by the recipient.

2. Assemble the trims as a separate one-piece "collage" so it can be removed for a keepsake or reused on another gift. Begin by pleating a small length of ribbon. Hot glue it to the small cardboard circle. Tie twigs together with raffia fibers. Apply a small amount of hot glue about 1" from the end of these raffia ties and quickly slip the beads onto the raffia ties, holding them over the glue until it bonds. Charms, buttons, shells, miniature masks, and wooden figures can also be used. Glue the twigs to the pleated ribbon (Fig. 2).

3. Wrap the package with raffia ties, having the ends of the ties extending slightly off the package. Hot glue the cardboard base of the trim collage over the center of the package (Fig. 3). The recipient can easily pry off the small cardboard base to remove the trim collage, then cut or untie the raffia.

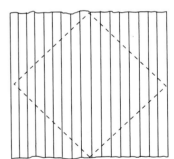

Fig. 1

Fig. 2

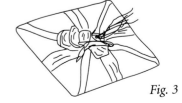

Fig. 3

When you're looking for the simplest way to a dramatic look, try these quick ideas for incorporating African fabrics into your home.

Turn a kente strip section into an interesting frame mat for a poster or photo.

Above: Use mudcloth as a bed coverlet. It requires only simple hemming, so the piece stays intact should you decide to use it for a specific project in the future. This red cloth is paired with an antique appliquéd pillow from India.

Left: Decorate your existing lamps, picture frames, etc. with African beads, cowrie shells, miniature masks, and so forth. In addition to shopping for them, don't overlook your jewelry box as a source of interesting trims (like broken strands of beads and unmatched earrings).

Choose a favorite African garment from your wardrobe and display it on a rod, similar to Japanese kimonos that are displayed as wall art. A stylized mannequin or retail display hanger can also be used, giving you the opportunity to enjoy the garment every day.

Make the room divider screens from a single fabric as an alternative to piecing a korhogo (see page 43), then add basic pillows (pages 40 to 42) in the same fabric as chair cushions for a designer touch.

For unique napkin rings, glue an ornament or large button onto a D-ring (sold in the sewing notions department), using hot glue or jewelry cement. Pair the napkin and ring with a coordinating "mudcloth" place mat you paint yourself!

SUPPLIES AND RESOURCES

General Supplies

Contact the companies listed in this section for information on the supplies used in this book.

AfriCraft–Authentic African Print Ribbon
P.O. Box 5214
Hillside, NJ 07205
800-568-7171
Fabric ribbons including plain edge, gold-edge, wire, and non-wire styles.

Aleene's
85 Industrial Way
Buellton, CA
800-825-3363
www.aleenes.com
Fabric laminates, stiffeners, and adhesives.

BagWorks
3301-C South Cravens Road
Fort Worth, TX 76119
817-446-8080
e-mail: tware@bagworks.com
www.bagworks.com
Canvas blanks (floorcloths, pillow covers, napkins).

Beacon Adhesives/Signature Crafts
P.O. Box 427
Wycoff, NJ 07481
800-TO KRAFT (800-865-7238)
Fabric laminates, stiffeners, and adhesives.

Calico Moon Handcrafts
www.boxabilities.com
800-678-7607
Kits for cardboard boxes (including the Crescent Moon box).

Celebrations of America
P.O. Box 280
Pottsville, AR 72858
501-967-1212
Compressed sponges for adinkra stamping.

Chronicle Books
85 Second Street
San Francisco, CA 94105
415-537-3730
Mini adinkra rubber stamp set perfect for greeting cards, stationery, etc.

The Crowning Touch
3859 South Stage Road
Medford, OR 97501
541-772-8430
FasTurn tube turning tool. Turn fabric tubes right-side-out and stuff them all in one step.

Design 1
P.O. Box 1508
Richmond, CA 94802
800-253-9900
Muslin dolls in a range of sizes, shapes, and skintone colors.

Dharma Trading Co.
P.O. Box 150916
San Rafael, CA 94915
415-456-7657
www.dharmatrading.com
Textile craft supplies catalog (dyes, paints, canvas blanks, etc.) includes compressed sponge sheets for adinkra stamping and Liquitex paints.

Fiber City Sewing
775 West Jackson Boulevard
Chicago, IL 60661
312-648-0954
Euro-Pro ironing system.

Home Arts
1979 Falcon Ridge Drive
Petaluma, CA 94954
888-639-8570
www.svn.net/homearts
Kits for cardboard boxes, picture frames, tissue boxes, etc.

Homeland Authentics
122 West 27th Street, 8th Floor
New York, NY 10001
800-AFRICAN
www.homeland-ibn.com
Authentic African prints, mudcloth, wovens. Also available: garments, home and fashion accessories, and hand-crafted gift items. Color catalog available.

HTC
Consumer Products Division
60 Metro Way
Secaucus, NJ 07094
www.htc-inc.net
Fusible products (Trans-Web, Fusible Fleece, etc.) and stabilizers and SpaceBoard multi-purpose work surface.

Kreinik
3106 Timanus Lane, Suite 101
Baltimore, MD 21244
800-354-4255
Pure silk threads (various styles and weights).

Liquitex/Binney & Smith Inc.
1100 Church Lane, P.O. Box 431
Easton, PA 18044-0431
610-253-6272
Acrylic paints, varnishes, and floorcloth finishes.

Loose Ends
3824 River Road North
Keizer, OR 97303
503-390-7457
www.4loosends.com
Project Papers, raffia, and other interesting natural grass fiber products. Fun, exotic accents for almost any African fabric project.

Mission Valley Textiles, Inc.
980 6th Avenue
New York, NY 10018
212-382-5455
Yarn-dyed plaids, ikats, and dobby weaves. Coordinate well with bright African prints.

One World Button Supply
41 Union Square, Room 311
New York, NY 10003
212-691-1331
Buttons, charms, and accents from sources worldwide. Specializing in glass, horn, shell, wood, and other natural materials.

Rubber Stampede
P.O. Box 246
Berkeley, CA 94701
510-420-6800
www.rubberstampede.com
Rubber stamps ("Primitives")

The Unique Spool
407 Corte Majorca
Vacaville, CA 95688
707-448-1538
African fabric prints. Also patterns for African-themed wall hangings, dolls, and crafts.

Viking Sewing Machine Co.
31000 Viking Parkway
Westlake, OH 44145
440-808-6550
www.husqvarnaviking.com
Viking 1+ sewing machine

Walnut Hollow
1409 State Road 23
Dodgeville, WI 53533-2112
800-950-5101
Clock faces and components, unfinished wood benches, etc.

Fabric Resources

The availability of Afrocentric fabrics and accessories is constantly increasing. Listed below are some valuable resources to check when shopping for or studying African textiles and related items:

Afritex
350 7th Avenue, Suite 1701
New York, NY 10001
888-9AFRITEX
e-mail: info@afritex.com
Contemporary African prints, printed mudcloth, brocades. Swatchbook available.

As-Hro Fabrics
2748 Wisconsin Street
Downers Grove, IL 60515
800-532-7476
Mudcloth, korhogos, wovens, printed leather, and silk. Minimums apply, or call for local retailers.

G Street Fabrics
Mail Order Service
12240 Wilkins Avenue
Rockville, MD 20852
800-333-9191
(There are also four store locations in Maryland and Virginia.)

Harlem Market
116th St. (between Malcolm X Blvd. and 5th Ave.)
New York, NY
212-987-8131
A unique uptown NYC open-air market featuring African fabrics, masks and other crafts, trims, and specialty items. Vendors represent more than fifteen countries.

Harlem Textile Works
186 East 122 Street
New York, NY 10035
212-534-3377
Original handprinted fabrics, home textiles, stationery. Special programs including custom screenprinting. Fabric swatches are available. Tours of the facility can be arranged.

Homeland Authentics
122 West 27th Street
New York, NY 10001
800-AFRICAN
African prints, mudcloth, korhogos, plus imported home furnishings, apparel, and gift items. Catalog available.
*Selected Homeland fabrics are sold through Hancock Fabrics and JoAnn Fabrics nationwide. Please check your local telephone directory for the store nearest you.

Kaarta Imports
121 West 125th Street
New York, NY 10027
212-866-5190
Fax 212-665-9815
African prints, large selection of mudcloth and korhogo, beads, apparel. Minimums apply for phone and mail orders.

Tunde Dada House of Africa (Four locations in NJ/NY metro area)
356 Main Street
Orange, NJ 07050-2703
973-673-4446
African fabrics, gifts, books, home furnishings, art, toys, and apparel.

Catalog and Internet Resources

Adire African Textiles Gallery
www.adire.clara.net
e-mail: duncan@adire.clara.net
Author Duncan Clarke offers information on adinkra, kente, mudcloth, kuba, and more, along with pieces for sale. He also sells cloth and trimmings in London at the Portobello Road Market in London.

African Crafts Online
www.africancrafts.com
Unique site "dedicated to brining the arts and artisans of Africa online." Showcases work of contemporary African artists. Books, shopping, and online postcards.

African American Shopping Mall
www.aasm.com
Includes vendors of African crafts, books, textiles, and more.

AfricanFabrics.com
www.africanfabrics.com
770-996-3106
Includes African prints and novelty fabrics and gallery of creative ideas. There is also a retail store in Riverdale, Georgia.

The Black Market
www.theblackmarket.com
Includes vendors of African crafts, books, textiles, and more.

Gold Coast Africa
www.goldcoastafrica.com
800-818-5136
Gifts and home furnishings. Catalog available.

Kente Cloth Festival
www.kente.net
212-481-2481 (NYC showroom)
Authentic kente cloth, garments, and custom design services.

Tunde Dada House of Africa
www.tundedada.com
African gifts, art, books, fabrics, and decor items.

Resource Advantage
www.rasource.com/ethnicafrican.html
A listing of multicultural specialty sources in New York City, from retailers to museums to special venues.

Special Resources

Ashanti Origins
1025 Connecticut Avenue NW, Suite 1012
Washington, DC 20036
202-857-9799
e-mail: ashantiorigins@hotmail.com
This distinctive custom furniture collection combines traditional and modern design, incorporating natural materials. Wood, iron, brass, leather, cloth, and materials indigenous to Ghana are used. These "furniture as art" pieces include chairs, lamps, mirrors, shelves, CD racks, bed, and lounger, each hand-crafted and made to order.

Bandele Publications
P.O. Box 21540
Washington, DC 20009
301-779-7530
e-mail: bandele@erols.com
Educational charts and posters explaining the symbolism in African textiles and culture, including kente and adinkra symbols. Detailed information makes these perfect for classroom settings as well as general research and enjoyment.

Costume and Textile Collection
Fashion Institute of Technology
Seventh Avenue @ 27 Street
New York, NY 10001
212-217-7700
Extensive research and study resources for museum members, including swatchbooks.

Dover Publications
31 East 2nd Street
Mineola, NY 11501
Publishes *African Designs from Traditional Sources* and other educational reference books. Designs are available for use by private individuals. This is a great source of ideas for making your own African-inspired fabrics and crafts.

"Sewing with Mudcloth"
P.O. Box 3276
Falls Church, VA 22043-3276
Designer and author Ronke Luke-Boone gives practical tips and creative suggestions for using mudcloth in apparel sewing, but most of the information applies to home decor sewing as well. Useful information from selection to sewing to care methods. Also available: "Sewing with Fancy Prints" and sewing patterns for apparel.

Stemmer House Publishers, Inc.
2627 Caves Road
Owings Mills, MD 21117
Publishes *African Printed Textile Designs* as well as other art design reference books, with designs available for use by private individuals. A great source of designs for making your own versions of African fabrics.

Museums and Organizations

ATA–Aid to Artisans
14 Brick Walk Lane
Farmington, CT 06032
860-677-1649
www.aid2artisans.org
Non-profit group providing practical assistance to artisans worldwide, forming partnerships to preserve artistic traditions and community well-being through training, product development, production, and marketing.

Fowler Museum of Cultural History at UCLA
P.O. Box 951549
Los Angeles, CA 90095
310-824-4361
www.ucla.edu
Includes extensive holding of African textiles and educational resources.

The National Museum of African Art (Smithsonian)
950 Independence Avenue SW
Washington, DC 20560
202-357-4600
www.si.edu/nmafa
Permanent and varying exhibits; museum shop carries home furnishings, some fabrics, crafts, books, etc.

The Newark Museum
49 Washington Street
Newark, NJ 07101-0540
973-596-6550
Catalog available from the 1998 exhibit "Wrapped in Pride: Ghanaian Kente and African American Pride". Also publishes an annual African Textiles calendar.

The Textile Museum
2320 S Street NW
Washington, DC 20008-4088
202-667-0441
www.textilemuseum.org
Varying exhibits and vast educational and research resources including a mail-order book list.

GLOSSARY

Abstract: A design that is freeform, not representing a particular object.

Appliqué: A fabric cut-out that is applied to a larger piece of fabric in a decorative manner.

Ashanti (also Asante): A large Ghanaian cultural group who developed and perfected such textile arts as kente strip weaving and adinkra stamping.

Bamana: A group in Mali whose skills in creating mudcloth are traditionally passed from mother to daughter.

Baste: To hand-sew, using long, loose stitches. Holds layers of fabric in place until more permanent stitching is added.

Bullion fringe: A standard home decor trim made of thick, twisted strands of rayon or cotton. Makes excellent "braided" doll hair in black, brown, beige, and other colors.

Buttonhole twist: A very heavy machine sewing thread, useful for creating a more visible outline around appliqués.

Calabash: A gourd or hard shell that is carved into a variety of household objects throughout Western Africa, including adinkra stamps.

Caustic soda: A strong solution that acts as a mordant in the production of mudcloth. It bleaches out the design areas of the cloth, leaving the dark mud in the background.

Circumference: The measurement completely around a circle.

Compressed sponge: A type of sponge that is firmly compacted for simplified cutting of stamp shapes. When dipped in water, it expands to regular sponge form.

Cording: Any narrow tie that can be made from raffia, cotton, rayon, silk, or synthetics, used as a decorative or functional accent, such as a drawstring.

Corrugated cardboard: A firm paperboard with support ridges running lengthwise.

Cowrie shells: Usually ivory in color, but also black and brown, these decorative shells were once used as currency. Widely symbolic of African culture in general, especially popular in jewelry.

Crosshatching: A fill pattern that consists of two sets of lines drawn close together, crossing over each other, usually diagonally.

Cut-pile: The fuzzy, raised design areas of a Kasaï velvet, or any other piled fabric such as dress velvet or corduroy.

Diameter: The measurement across the widest part of a circle.

Distress: To give craft paper a beaten, weathered, or aged look through dampening and wrinkling.

Double-heddle: A type of weaving loom with two sets of pulleys used to raise and lower the warp yarns, allowing for more intricate patterns than a single heddle loom.

Double-needle: A decorative machine stitch using a special machine needle with two eyes, feeding through two spools of thread simultaneously, resulting in two rows of evenly spaced stitching.

Dyestuff: A complex mixture of various dyes, mordants, and other ingredients, used to color and decorate textiles and other objects.

Embroider: A method of decorating a fabric by hand or machine stitching it with contrasting thread (usually heavier weight).

Fabric stiffening spray: A textile finish that gives added body to a finished project, helping it to keep its intended shape.

Fermentation: The process in which a dye breaks down chemically. In the case of mud dyes made for mudcloth or korhogo, this results in a darker color of dyestuff than the original.

Fill patterns: The various decorative ink strokes artists use to fill in areas of a korhogo design, including thick or thin lines, dots, and solid areas.

Fixative fabric spray: A textile finish that sets the dyes in a fabric to help prevent it from bleeding.

Floral foam: A moldable foam, usually green or faded brown, into which flower stems are inserted to stabilize a floral arrangement.

Fusible: A no-sew craft item that is applied to fabric with the heat of an iron. When a fusible is bonded to a fabric, the bond is meant to be permanent.

Fusible craft backing: A layer of nonwoven material that remains in the project, acting as a stabilizer or stiffener. It is ironed to the wrong side of the fabric. Available in various weights.

Fusible fleece: Craft padding (approximately 1/4" thick) with fusible web applied to one side. Can be used for picture frames, photo albums, quilts, etc.

Fusible hem tape: Fusible web sold on a roll (usually 3/4" wide), convenient for hems, applying trims, and similar applications.

Fusible web (such as Stitch Witchery): A thin material placed between two layers of fabric to join them without sewing. The paper-backed version allows you to apply the web to one fabric first, peel the paper away, then iron this fabric to the second one. The paper protects your iron from contact with the sticky web. Unlike fusible craft backing, fusible web melts into the fabric layers, disappearing as it bonds them.

Gesso: A liquid sealer applied to a fabric before it is painted, which prevents paints from being absorbed into the fabric, maintaining their full color vibrancy. Used in preparation for floorcloth painting.

Indigenous: Originating, growing in, or naturally occurring in a particular environment, such as the natural dyes used to color mudcloth or korhogos.

Juxtaposition: The careful placement of an intricate mix of patterns, colors, and designs in a Kasaï velvet arrangement. The more varied the juxtaposition, the higher the aesthetic value.

Kuba: A central African culture known for its embroidered and appliquéd raffia cloths.

Lightfastness: A fabric's ability to resist fading when exposed to sunlight.

Liquid laminate: Clear-drying adhesive used to adhere fabric or paper to clear surfaces like plastic or glass. Apply smoothly to eliminate air bubbles, making the laminate as invisible as possible.

Manufactured mudcloth: The mass-produced fabric that mimics the designs found in authentic mudcloth. Produced in Africa as well as other parts of the world.

Mordant: A chemical or other additive that fixes a dye, protecting it from fading in light and permitting some level of washability. Cream of tartar and alum are commonly used as mordants.

Motif: A design, shape, or symbol used to decorate a textile or other object.

Mottled: A painted effect that results in various shades of a color, giving a softer, slightly aged, or weathered effect as compared to a solid color.

Muted: A faded, washed-out, or softened version of a color.

Particle board: Strong but flexible wood product used in crafting. Available in the lumber department of home improvement centers.

Piping: Decorative cording that is inserted between two layers of fabric, as found on the edges of sheets and pillow cases.

Plexiglas: Acrylic plastic sheeting used for crafting as well as inexpensive replacement windows. Found in home improvement centers.

Raffia: Fibers pulled from the stalks of palm trees, then woven, pounded, dyed, and otherwise processed for use as decoration, apparel, and even currency.

Rod pocket: The section along the top edge of a wall hanging that is folded to the back and stitched down, allowing a hanging rod to slip inside.

Right sides together: A basic sewing term describing a seam joining two pieces of fabric, where the right sides of the fabric face each other as they are stitched.

Rights-of-passage: Cultural ceremonies or events that mark milestones in one's life, such as the transition from childhood to adulthood.

Rub-off: A method of transferring a pattern from one surface to another. A symbol is photocopied, the back of the photocopy is rubbed with pencil lead, then this sheet is placed right side up over the second surface. The symbol is then traced over, leaving a pencil lead tracing on the second surface.

Scoring: Placing careful cuts scarcely halfway through the thickness of a cardboard, allowing it to bend cleanly without splitting. Always score the side of the cardboard that is opposite the side you want to bend.

Seam sealant (such as FrayCheck): A clear adhesive that is applied sparingly to the cut edge of a fabric to prevent it from raveling.

Self-binding: A narrow strip of fabric used to finish the edge of a wall hanging or other project, taken from the fabric of the project itself.

Senufo: A people of the Ivory Coast who developed the art of korhogo painting, a dramatic look that features stylized animal and human figures.

Shuttle: A stick around which yarn is wound, the shuttle is passed back and forth by a weaver to create the weft of the fabric while the warp yarns are raised and lowered. Used in kente strip weaving.

Slipstitch: A basic sewing term describing small, neat hand stitches used to close an opening, such as a pillow. The stitches should be as invisible as possible.

Spanish moss: A material resembling dried, faded grass; used as an overall filler at the base of a floral arrangement.

Spot fuse: Fusing temporarily with a light touch of the corner of an iron to check placement or measurements before fusing a project permanently.

Tea-dye: A method of coloring a fabric to give it an aged look.

Textile medium: A liquid that is added to craft paints when used on fabrics to help them penetrate more readily and reduce the stiffening effect of the paint on the fabric.

Topstitch: Machine stitching that is placed close to the edge of a fabric, with the right side of the fabric facing up on the sewing machine.

Tufts: The tiny, individual cuts of raffia or other fiber that, together, result in a cut-pile effect.

Varnish: A protective liquid finish applied to a painted fabric. Generally available in matte, satin, and glossy finishes.

Warp: The vertical yarns of a woven fabric.

Weft: The horizontal yarns of a woven fabric (these run "weft to right").

Wire-edge ribbon: A craft trim with thin wire running along both edges, so that the ribbon can be molded into any form.

Wrapper: The generic term for a basic garment worn by men and women throughout Africa. Can be kente, adinkra, Kuba cloth, or other fabrications.

Bibliography

Adler & Barnard. *African Majesty—The Textile Art of the Ashanti and the Ewe*. London: Thames and Hudson Ltd., 1992.

Adinkra Symbolism Chart. Distributed by Bandele Publications, Washington, DC. Published by Sankofa Publications, Hyattsville, MD, 1978. Revised 1993.

Barnard, Nicholas. *Living With Decorative Textiles*. London: Thames and Hudson Ltd., 1989.

Clarke, Duncan. *The Art of African Textiles*. London: Promotional Reprint Co., 1997.

Corbin, George A. *Native Arts of North America, Africa and the South Pacific*. New York: Harper & Row, 1988.

Horn, Diane V. *African Printed Textile Designs*. Owings Mills, MD: Stemmer House, 1996.

Kuchinsky, Caroline. *Fabulous Floorcloths*. Iola, WI: Krause Publications, 1998.

Lamb, Venice and Alistair. *West African Strip Weaving*. Washington, DC: The Textile Museum, 1995.

Luke-Boone, Ronke. *Sewing with Mudcloth*. Falls Church, VA: 1998.

Meyer, Laure. *Art and Craft in Africa*. Paris: Terrail, 1995.

Newman, Thelma R. *Contemporary African Arts and Crafts*. New York: Crown Publishers, Inc., 1974.

Picton, John. *The Art of African Textiles: Technology, Tradition and Lurex*. London: Lund Humphries Publishers, 1995.

Rovine, Victoria. *African Textiles & Adornments*. Univ. of Iowa Museum of Art, 1995.

Sieber, Roy. *African Textiles and Decorative Arts*. Museum of Modern Art, 1972.

West African Textiles and Dress. Exhibition Guide, Kent State University.

Williams, Geoffrey. *African Designs from Traditional Sources*. Mineola, NY: Dover Publications, 1971.

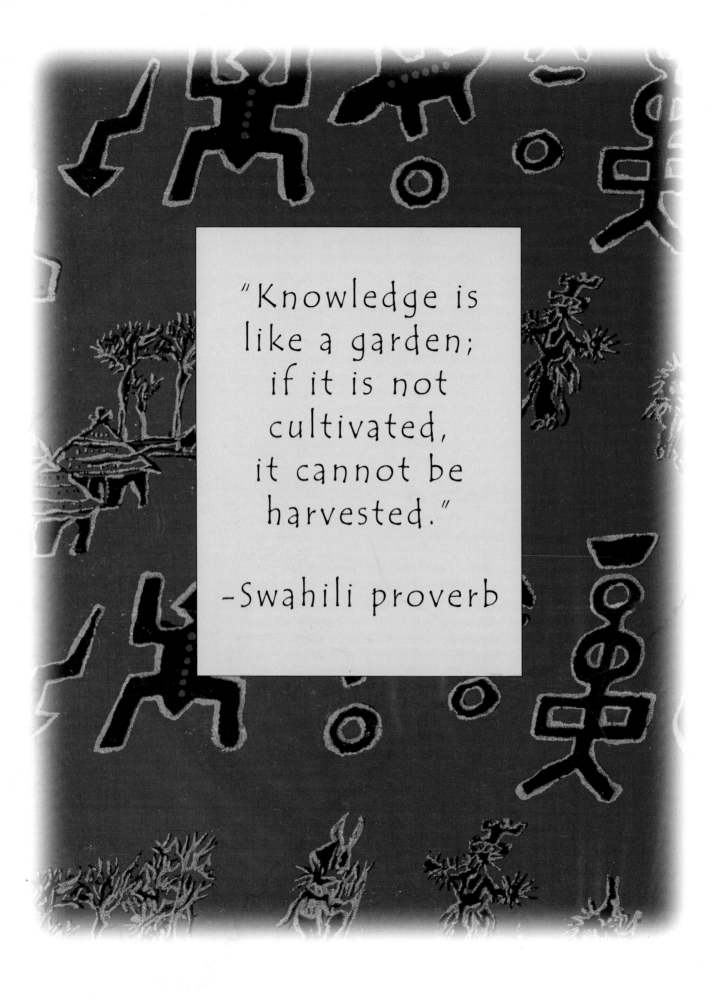

"Knowledge is like a garden; if it is not cultivated, it cannot be harvested."

-Swahili proverb